To Dreamers Long Forgotten

BY TIM WHITE

FOREWORD BY
ROBERT A. SCHULLER

For information contact:

WASHINGTON CATHEDRAL
12300 Woodinville-Redmond Road N.E.
Redmond, WA 98052

Cover and Interior Design © 2005 TLC Graphics
www.TLCGraphics.com

ISBN: 0-9763367-0-7

Printed in the United States of America

DEDICATION

This book is dedicated to Ruth Apted, Marcy Marquez, Earl Snyder, Marvin Stone, and most of all, Jane Bishop, who typed the first draft of this manuscript. We grew very close as we adventured together on the battlefield of a great dream. I witnessed their wisdom and celebrated their uniqueness, and I shared in the luminous meaning of their lives until they took their last breath. Someday we will all rejoice together in the great celebration. They are dreamers I will never forget, and their stories reflect the grandeur often overlooked in the quiet people who stand up for their ideals, unannounced but not unforgotten.

FOREWORD

Tim White introduced himself to me in 1984 when he invited me to come to his church. He asked me to inspire his congregation and motivate them to express the love of God in their lives. I accepted the invitation.

When I arrived at the Seattle airport and met Tim for the first time, I was immediately impressed with his positive attitude, his child-like faith, and his explosive enthusiasm.

While in Seattle, he filled me in on the details of my appearance:

1. The "church" had only been meeting for five months.
2. Their congregation was about 50 strong.
3. They didn't have a church building.
4. I would be speaking in a gymnasium.
5. One thousand people were expected to attend.

How they could expect 1,000 people when they only had a congregation of 50 was beyond me. But I was there. The following day I would address the congregation of 50 or 1,000.

Tim's attitude, faith, and enthusiasm must have been contagious because on Sunday morning, June 9, 1985, his efforts were rewarded. After the last child was counted, the total attendance record showed 1,001 persons in attendance.

From that point, Tim's ministry has flourished. Because of his vision and dream, Washington Cathedral is alive today.

Tim's success is a result of years of training, which goes back three generations.

In 1973 Reverend Tim White was called into the Christian ministry. His call came from God, who used two great men to inspire him: his father and his grandfather. Tim's call represents an unbroken succession of three generations of ordained Christian ministers.

The Bible refers to God's blessings being passed to "your children and your children's children." Tim is a living example of God's blessing being poured out upon the life of one of his children, Floyd Edward White. Even after his physical death in 1989, God kept His promise to him.

Tim's grandfather was born in the late 1890s as what was then called an illegitimate child. He was living on his own on the streets by the age of 10. He came back from fighting in World War I determined to invest his life in following Christ and the revolution of love and faith. He served in 13 country churches for 55 years with a positive faith through the Great Depression, World War II, the Korean conflict, and the Vietnam War.

This book is about Floyd Edward White, whom God has blessed. Tim shares with us the valuable lessons he learned from his grandfather...lessons that are timeless and priceless.

Tim White has been a close friend of mine for many years, and I consider it a privilege and an honor to be invited to introduce this book to you. It is my hope that this book will bless you and your children and your children's children.

Robert A. Schuller

TABLE OF CONTENTS

Preface
◄ ix ►

Chapter One
*The Visitor From
Another Century*
◄ 1 ►

Chapter Two
*A Cold River
Called Loneliness*
◄ 15 ►

Chapter Three
Growing Up Alone
◄ 25 ►

Chapter Four
*I Will Lift Mine Eyes
Unto The Hills*
◄ 41 ►

Chapter Five

*The Friend That Sticketh
Closer Than A Brother*

◁ 61 ▷

Chapter Six

The Miracle of Love

◁ 75 ▷

Chapter Seven

*People Who Hate God and the
Pastor Who Loved Them*

◁ 95 ▷

Chapter Eight

*Tough Times, Tough People,
and Their Pastor*

◁ 113 ▷

Chapter Nine

Heart Wounds

◁ 139 ▷

Chapter Ten

Lessons From Grandpa

◁ 157 ▷

Preface

> *"I bethought myself of my preface I was to make
> to Don Quixote's history, which did so much trouble
> me as I neither meant to make any at all,
> nor publish the acts of so noble a knight."*

CERVANTES, *The Ingenious Gentleman*
Don Quixote De La Mancha, 1605 AD

This is a story of the twentieth century, told through the adventures of a common man who lived, loved, and dreamed during that wonderful century. His life began in the nineteenth century before the advent of the airplane, automobile, telephone, radio, television, computer, or national income tax.

When he was a child, the Apache chief Geronimo was still alive.

When he was growing up, the oldtimers told proud narratives of battle scars and their tragic memories of the Civil War.

When he was a man, he watched Neil Armstrong walk on the moon.

When he held his great-grandchildren, Vietnam veterans hid their heroism, not knowing how they would be accepted.

This is the saga of a rural society that was forever transformed in one century by powerful, sweeping social crucibles. No one could have entirely envisioned World War I, the Great

Depression, or World War II. Common opinion certainly could not predict the dramatic restructuring of society under the pressures of advancing science and unexpected world events.

This is the story of a common ordinary man, his adventures in the twentieth century, and the legacy he left his loved ones. The story is so extravagantly common, that if you will but open the package, it will reflect the birthright presented to you from your forefathers. This cleverly wrapped inheritance will make your adventure a bit easier as you explore the uncharted waters of the twenty-first century.

Like many of our legacy gifts, this one is wrapped in the story of a "nobody" who began his life as a nobody and ended his life as a dreamer who never saw his dreams fulfilled. He was quixotic, and wondered if he ever had an impact upon others. More than anything else, he was a human being with imperfections, doubts, and haunting mistakes. Yet at the same time, he was a human being who loved other people in spite of their imperfections, doubts, and haunting mistakes. And how he loved!

He was totally a human, fully a dreamer, and completely an idealist! "Nobody" is a hard word to use to describe such a man, and I don't use it recklessly. This is the term he used to describe himself. I suspect he was trying to make a valuable point. He did that. He left subtle points that would often take years to discover. Maybe everyone does, if we would just learn to listen.

Floyd Edward White was a simple country pastor. I guess you could call him a "nobody" pastor. He shepherded "nobodies" in small farming communities, and he never made much money. In fact, his family felt resentment because of the little he earned.

He lived a hard life during difficult times, but he made it all a little easier for the other "nobodies" who were graced to be his friends. He was like many ordinary people you could hardly call great in historical terms. That is, not great unless you carefully observe their lives to discover the epic human drama, the bold quest for real growth, and the resolution of terrible conflict between the good and evil that must do battle in every human, every community, and every generation.

He ministered in so many different farming communities, that unless you talk to a character who enjoys the worn-out tales of the old-timers, it's hard to find someone today who remembers him. It goes without saying that he was never a celebrity, except to his family and friends. He never had a book published, but he did print his own collection of stories and jokes. There is probably not a living person who remembers very much of any of his sermons, although he gave his life to preaching an encouraging message, week after week for 55 years.

Ralph Waldo Emerson understood the hidden treasure in the simple people of life. He commented on this discovery in his essay on *The Over-Soul*.

> *Converse with a mind that is grandly simple, and literature looks like word-catching. The simplest utterances are worthiest to be written, yet are they so cheap, and so things of course, that in the infinite riches of the soul, it is like gathering a few pebbles off the ground, or bottling a little air in a phial, when the whole earth, and the whole atmosphere are ours.*

Floyd Edward White was that kind of a grandly simple man. This is a true story told to me by Floyd and Ione White, who were my grandparents. Grandma was struggling with impending death from cancer, and Grandpa prayed that the Lord would take him quickly after Grandma, as he could not bear to live without her.

As I type this book, I have his collected sermons sitting beside me in a shoebox. Some of them are dated 1938 or 1956. I recall talking with him one day after I had read the collection. "Grandpa," I told him with tears in my eyes, "you were a great preacher!" He spoke to me proudly, but also with tears in his eyes. "Well, I worked hard at it." He never won any awards, and he never spoke to a large crowd. The number of people who felt responsible to tell him "thank you" were very few... but he didn't care about that very much.

Both Grandpa and Grandma White had a knack for telling stories. When I first approached them about telling me their story, they both trembled and looked at each other as if they were embarrassed to reveal their dreams, failings, and most profound conflicts. This may have been almost impossible to disclose, except to a grandchild at a deathbed. Maybe they were free to divulge their story to me because my dream was to be a country pastor in the city. Then again, maybe it was simply because I asked at the right time. This would be the first and last time that they would let down their guard to unveil the very best stories, which had remained untold through three generations.

It is a matter of historical record that there is no reliable historical record about Grandpa's age. Another way to put it would be like this — there is no historical record of Grandpa's age that would not bring up a serious family disagreement. All we know for sure is that he was born in another century, in Arkansas, and was nearing 100 years of age when he finally "sang" himself to death. That phrase may sound peculiar, but that is exactly what he did. Over a period of 16 months, he was expected to die at any moment. During that time, the pattern would be for him to go into a coma, repeatedly. He wanted to die, and the family was ready for him to die. The only problem was that he would start singing the old hymns of his faith. It was haunting in the middle of the night to hear Grandpa in his dark bedroom singing, *I'd Rather Have Jesus Than Silver and Gold* or *I Love to Tell the Story*. It would almost sound like someone else was in there with him. He was totally oblivious to any conversation from this world. After hours and hours of singing, he would come out giggling and laughing, as though he knew some grand joke that none of the rest of us could understand. There were even times when he had not walked in months and after one of these spells he would walk out of his room as though he were 15 years younger! His sharp mind would again be with him. For a while we thought he simply had too much faith to die. When he finally did pass on, he sang and sang as if he were in another century. He opened his eyes for the first time in days and looked around the room at his beloved family, wearing the biggest smile of his life. Then he just closed his eyes and breathed quieter and quieter, until he was no longer there.

This is the story of Floyd and Ione White the way they told it to me when Grandma was on her deathbed. The three of us shared again the events of their lives, and at times it was as if they were reliving these adventures. As they told the story, they dialogued with unseen ghosts in the room. Tears were shed and belly laughs were heard, and I learned something about life I want to share with you.

Before I begin the story, it is important that I clarify some language that will be used later in the book. As Grandpa told me about his childhood, he remembered conversations in which severe profanity was used against him. He did not use a lot of it, although he made it clear there was more used at the time than he was relating in the re-telling of the story. One reason this was so shocking to me was that in the 30 plus years I had known my grandparents, I had never known them to tolerate profanity. They were devout Evangelical Christians. In fact, normally Grandpa would have been taking his life in his hands to use such words in the presence of Grandma. But he told the story that way for a reason. It is my guess he knew of no other way to illustrate the deep personal hurt he had felt as those words were used against him. As a pastor myself, I do not repeat these words easily. However, I lacked any other way to describe the devastation to a young boy's self-worth and the distance created in relationships without quoting the language that was repeated to me. I do not believe my grandfather would have used such hard words unless it was essential to make the point that God had somehow reached down and healed his hidden, festering, emotional, and spiritual wounds.

The other factor to be considered in understanding this story is that Grandma was the stronger personality of the two. More of the narrative was her retelling of Grandpa's story than it was Grandpa telling his own version. That is to say, when there was an argument about the details, she always won.

This biography is not filled with historical facts. Floyd Edward White was not that kind of a character. For that very reason, it captures something of the wonder of life. If the story at times seems a little incoherent and protective of certain hurts, that is the way they told it to me. Therefore, I could write nothing more, or less. If it seems detailed in spots and vague at others, please understand that it was passed to me this way. If in some places it may sound as if they were trying to make a point, it is probably because they were. This story may seem too simplistic, from the perspective of our complex, modern society. But consider that this was the only way the profound message of my grandpa could be approached.

The story is intentionally naive as it comes through the triad of a plebeian grandfather, a cogent grandmother, and an adoring grandson. It should be taken as nothing more or less than that. I hope it is at least accepted as a biography for no other reason than it comes in the tradition of Mark Twain's biographical lead. It was Mark Twain who said while dictating his autobiography:

Within the last eight or ten years I have made several attempts to do the autobiography in one way or another with a pen, but the result was not satisfactory; it was too literary. With the pen in one's hand, narrative is a difficult art; narrative should flow as flows the brook down through the hills and the leafy woodlands, its course changed by every boulder it comes across and by every grass-clad gravelly spur that projects into its path; its surface broken, but its course not stayed by rocks and gravel on the bottom in the shallow places; a brook that never goes straight for a minute, but goes, and goes briskly, sometimes ungrammatically, and sometimes fetching a horseshoe three-quarters of a mile around, and at the end of the circuit flowing within a yard of the path it traversed an hour before; but always going and always following at least one law, always loyal to that law, the law of narrative, which has no law. Nothing to do but make the trip; the how of it is not important, so that the trip is made.

That was how this story was told. Sometimes Grandpa would stop to quote Grandma poetry, and tears would run freely. Other times, there would be quite an argument as to the exact details. As they relived the story with me, I believe they began to see some of the grandeur that had been missed or forgotten when they lived it the first time. As they told me the story, they repeatedly used those painful words: "We were just nobodies."

I suppose that's true, unless you had met them, just as sure as it is also true of thousands of quiet heroes who are also nobodies unless you've met them and discovered the greatness of their lives. As you read this book, remember the words of Reinhold Niebuhr: "Any dream that is truly from God will be too great for one generation." The dreams that may seem insignificant and unnoticed in your life today will be magnified in the following generations. In fact, imagine that someday your grandchild may be writing a book about your journey with the same unbridled enthusiasm that I write this. Perhaps you will discover the hidden Promethean qualities in your life as you read this book.

Here's to all those *Dreamers Long Forgotten,* and to those of us who choose to follow the paths they have blazed.

*Rev. Floyd
and Ione
White*

*Three Generations
Rev. Tim, Dale
and Floyd White*

The White Cabin
Wallowa Mountains, Oregon

CHAPTER ONE

A Visitor From Another Century

1901

Speeders pay $10

May 11 Members of the Automobile Club of America were arrested today in Morristown, New Jersey, for breaking the speed limit. The drivers violated the posted 8-mile-an-hour ordinance during a cross-state race.

Chronicle of the 20th Century, Chronicle Publications, Mount Kisco, New York, 1987, page 27

Settlers given vast Indian lands

Aug. 9 Oklahoma Territory has grown by 2,080,000 acres overnight, and a lucky 6,500 homesteaders have staked their claims.

Chronicle of the 20th Century, Chronicle Publications, Mount Kisco, New York, 1987, page 30

Guglielmo Marconi sends message from England to Newfoundland

Dec. 12 The Italian physicist Guglielmo Marconi, who sent wireless telegraphic messages across the English Channel from Dover, England, to Boulogne, France, on March 29, 1899, repeated his experiment today over the Atlantic Ocean, a distance of 2,232 miles.

Chronicle of the 20th Century, Chronicle Publications, Mount Kisco, New York, 1987, page 34

A Visitor From Another Century

The Duke: Why are you poets so fascinated with madmen?

Cervantes: I suppose...we have much in common.

The Duke: You both turn your backs on life.

Cervantes: We both select from life what pleases us.

The Duke: A man must come to terms with life as it is!

Cervantes: I have lived nearly fifty years, and I have seen life as it is. Pain, misery, hunger...cruelty beyond belief. I have heard the singing from taverns and the moans from bundles of filth on the streets. I have been a soldier and seen my comrades fall in battle...or die more slowly under the lash in Africa. I have held them in my arms at the final moment. These were men who saw life as it is, yet they died despairing. No glory, no gallant last words...only their eyes filled with confusion, whimpering the question: "Why?" I do not think they asked why they were dying, but why they had lived. When life itself seems lunatic, who knows where madness lies? Perhaps to be too practical is madness. To surrender dreams — this may be madness. To seek treasure where there is only trash. Too much sanity may be madness. And maddest of all, to see life as it is and not as it should be!

— *Dale Wasserman, Man of La Mancha*

In the doorway, surrounded by light, stood a visitor from another century. It was Sunday morning, one thousand, nine hundred, eighty-five AD, and Sunday school was finishing and worship was about to begin in Richland, Washington. Richland is a small city in Washington State, famous for its production of plutonium. In fact, half of all the atomic weapons in the world have received their plutonium from Richland's Hanford area.

Overlooking the valley of the Columbia River and the surrounding towns is a 2-million-dollar cathedral, constructed mostly of glass. In the basement, teenagers are tapping their feet to Christian rock music. Their jeans have designer labels, and their language is "rad." On the walls of their Sunday school classroom are posters of pro-football star Curt Warner running a football, an Olympic gold medalist skiing a slope, and Garfield the cat proclaiming a line of wisdom. A pool table sits in the corner of the glassed-in, carpeted room. They are watching a music video, and the Christian rock star on the screen is wearing a leopard jacket. He is dancing and singing, and the message is really getting through to the teenagers.

It was at this moment, when the video was at its very best, that this 91-year-old man, wearing a black robe worn thin from Sundays long gone by, stepped into the classroom. Both the teenagers and the old man were a bit shocked and taken aback by each other. He had been born in another century—before the airplane or automobile, before the computer or the television. Famous Indian war chiefs were still alive when he was a boy, and that century was a long way from this present scene. If this cathedral and these teenagers had somehow been transported to his century, the people of that time would have suspected that these teenagers were aliens from the planet Mars. The representative of this lost century had a tall frame bent from age, but he held his head high. What little hair he had was now white. His skin was wrinkled from blistering sunny days during the summers of his life. The teenagers were equally astonished, for they lived in an insulated world where all the buildings were new, the utensils were plastic, the equipment was high-tech, and the language was avant-garde.

One of the junior high girls jumped. "God, you scared me!"

If the teenagers could have looked deeply into his eyes, they would have noticed how shocked and hurt he was that a girl would use the Lord's name in vain while she was in church. But they didn't notice, so he set about the all-important task of crossing the generations.

"Well," he said with an almost musical saintliness, "I guess I'm lost."

"You sure are," heckled a teenager with purple hair. "Aren't you looking for Rod Serling and *The Twilight Zone*?" The other kids joined in, "Nee, nee, nee, nee...." They sang the theme song to the old TV show that they had only seen as reruns.

"I'm looking for that new sanctuary," the old gentleman replied, as if he didn't notice their cruel humor. But if you really knew him, you could tell that it hurt him.

"It's right up the stairs," giggled a girl.

"I know that," he answered graciously. "I just can't find the stairs."

The boy with purple hair put his arm around the old pastor condescendingly as he said, "Listen, Reverend Magoo." The kids laughed out loud, but the pastor didn't understand that again they were referring to an out-of-date cartoon character. "You just go out in the hall take a left, a right, and then follow the crowd." The junior high Sunday school teacher stepped back into the class catching the last part of the directions. He moved close to the kids and whispered, "Reverend White can't make it up those stairs." Then he spoke louder as the old pastor turned up his hearing aid. "Just go down that hall, and through the gardens and follow the ramp."

I stepped in and interrupted, "Come on, Grandpa, I'll grab my robe and take you with me."

"Just a minute, Tim." His blue-gray eyes twinkled at me with new strength. "I need to give these kids a blessing." He walked over to the kid with purple hair, squeezing his elbow and loving him with those powerful steel-gray eyes that had been forged and polished by decades of sorrow and hope. The boy softened a little. The old pastor began to chuckle, as he thought of a joke. He tried to tell it, but it tickled him so much that he had trouble. "Did I ever tell you about the man who was riding on a plane for the first time?"

"No," said the kid, "but I've got a feeling that you're going to tell me right now." Grandpa's head bobbled as he chuckled hard. "I love this one. You see, the stewardess gave chewing gum to the passengers to keep their ears from popping when the plane reached high altitudes. After the plane landed, a worried-looking man came to the hostess and said, 'That was my first flight, and it was nice, but now that it's over, how do I get the gum out of my ears?" Grandpa laughed so loud and hard we were all a little concerned for his health.

The boy with purple hair smiled. "How old are you anyway, Reverend White?"

The pastor could tell that he was making a friend, and he glowed as he answered, "Well, I don't know exactly, but I'm in my nineties."

Now the boy was trying to cross the generations as he commented, "Well, I hope I can be there for your 100th birthday."

"Why not?" said the old minister. "You'll make it; you look healthy enough to me." This time they all laughed and smiled.

As we were laughing, the mood in Grandpa's face began to change. He was glowing. No, I mean it, he was really glowing! I always wondered how he did that. He was glowing with love stronger than ever. He was still smiling, but a tear formed in his eye as he said the words that he had repeated for 55 years: "Shall we pray?" Then the pastor from a day gone by raised his hand above the heads of the children for a benediction as he prayed in a voice that seemed mighty strong to come from a little old man.

"God bless you, kids! You've got your whole lives ahead of you. Do something great for God! And now, dare to follow Jesus Christ! Be Christians. Where there is dark despair — give bright hope, where there is cold loneliness — give warm friendship; where there is crushing discouragement — give strong encouragement. Where there is —,"

"Reverend White," the lady's voice interrupted as we all opened our eyes from that magical moment. "Reverend White, the service is about to begin and your son, Pastor Dale, asked me to come and get you."

He appeared undisturbed by this suggestion, as his service had already begun. The old pastor turned and smiled. "That's all right. My grandson will bring me along as soon as I tell another joke."

As we walked on the ramp through the gardens, Grandpa raised his arm in full appreciation of the morning. "Well, look at this day, will you! It's just the kind of day we ought to have on a Sunday. The Lord always knows. The wonder of it all…the dew on the roses, the birds chirping, and the people coming to worship Almighty God. Look at the smiles on their beautiful faces. They know that they are going to meet Him. Oh, look at that couple over there. They really need God's love right now, I can sense it in my spirit…and God is just the kind to give it to them. Let's pray for them right now."

"Grandpa, the entire service is waiting for us," I pleaded.

That brought a big, beautiful smile as he said, "Well, isn't that wonderful, that's the way a worship service should be. Especially on a day like this!" He raised his arm again, but this time his palm was facing the dignified couple walking toward the sanctuary. He prayed with a loud voice that sounded something like Moses, or at least Charlton Heston: "Almighty God, Creator of the Universe, Loving Savior, bless that couple, and bless us so that we can share your love with all of these beautiful people this morning!" The couple looked surprised, like they thought that Grandpa was throwing something at them…and he was.

The distinguished 52-year-old senior pastor of this cathedral, my dad, gave his dad a hug. "Dad, let's go. Isn't it a wonderful day to worship?" He went on, saying, "Dad, when you say the prayer this morning, would you try to leave me some time to preach? And do you think that you could leave out the jokes? People have a hard time getting back into the flow of worship."

Grandpa just kept shining as he said, "You know, Dale, I'm proud of you. Look at this beautiful cathedral. I remember the day you were born, and the older you get the more you look like yourself. I can see that day like it was today. You barely made it, you know, but I knew that if Almighty God saw fit to give you life that His hand would be upon you."

We all walked up to the great granite altar in our fashionable blue-gray robes. But Grandpa wore his black robe, and that robe was so unimpressive. It did not have doctoral stripes or a master's hood. Its dignity came from its age. When Grandpa wore it, you couldn't help but see the day and the world he had come from...a world of farms and neighbors. It was a hard day, and yet a simpler day. We all knelt at the altar, except Grandpa, who stood holding on to the altar. I looked up at him to see the sweat beading up on his forehead and his legs trembling to hold that position. It was impossible for him to kneel and then get back up again, so he struggled to hold this awkward position. It took the courage of an athlete for him to make it to the platform. He exercised all week to get up those stairs. It was now his moment and he stood before the congregation of over 1,000 people.

"In my day, a gentleman would never think of entering a church with a hat on, and here in the second row sits a man with a hat on." Everyone in the church turned red from embarrassment, because it was a lady to whom he was referring.

Grandpa just couldn't see that far. But Grandpa just smiled. He wasn't putting anyone down; he was simply making a point. "That goes to show you how styles and times have changed. I have seen so many changes: not one person rode a horse to church this morning. In fact, this church that has everything doesn't even have a place to keep horses. I'm glad I didn't ride my horse, 'Old Cap,' here this morning. Boy, do times change and in many ways people have changed to keep pace with the times. But Almighty God remains the same. He loves you and can help you today the same way He loved and helped the people in my day. The Good News of Jesus Christ is the same yesterday, today, and tomorrow!"

A power capsule
inspired by Matthew 25:21

*"His master replied, "Well done, good
and faithful servant! You have been faithful with
a few things; I will put you in charge of many things.
Come and share your master's happiness!"*

*If you cannot do great things yourself...
Dare to do small things in a great way!*

"Our heavenly Father," (people bobbed their heads not knowing whether he was praying or talking), "it's so good to be here and to sense your wonderful presence. Uh....uh....uh." Grandpa paused for a long time. I opened my eyes to see his hands trembling as he held the pulpit.

I prayed, "Please, Jesus, help Grandpa...he's drawing a blank again!" Finally, Grandpa continued, and I relaxed.

"And Lord, you know the one about the absent-minded professor who remembered there was something he wanted very much to do that night and he sat up late beating his brain to remember what it was. Around two o'clock in the morning it suddenly came to him. He wanted to go to bed early."

The crowd roared in laughter, lifting their heads and opening their eyes, thinking that the prayer was over. But the prayer was never over with Grandpa, not really. My dad looked at me with a smile on his face as if to say, "Grandpa always finds a way to work a joke in and I guess the Lord does know that one." But Grandpa was still praying, and everyone quickly bowed their heads and closed their eyes again.

"Oh Lord, that's funny when it's a professor but not when it's me. I worked all week on this prayer to lift these people to you and to shine your love to them and now I've lost it." You could hear a pin drop as Grandpa started another long uncomfortable pause. Finally he continued, "Well there's one thing I know. Each of you was created for a reason and the reason is now. Our gracious Master has given each of you a great job to do. Oh, it might not seem very great — my life doesn't seem so great...in fact today's society might call me a failure." The emotion in his voice cut to the heart of each listener as he was speaking straight from his heart. He continued with glory in his voice, "But when you dare to follow Jesus Christ and really love people, it's...it's wonderful! He is such a wonderful God, and he has given each of you a wonderful adventure to follow. You're just like a flower blossoming to give God glory. Whether you are a dirt farmer, a star athlete who's the best thing since sliced bread, a hard-working janitor, a struggling businessperson, or a simple grandmother — *You are the creation of Almighty God!* You may never be famous, but some of you may become very famous...I don't know. But I do know that either way, it's loving people that counts, and doing the best you can with what you've got. So no matter who we are, we need Jesus to teach us to love, and how to really live. That is why when we pray together…every one of us is a little lonely child in desperate need of help from The Almighty.

"Our Father, who art in heaven, hallowed be thy name. Thy kingdom come." Everyone began to get the idea to join in, and with our eyes closed we were children again in need of help from a living, loving God. It seemed that for a moment we were transported in time to another century — where things were simpler and they made sense, and the profundity of that simplicity almost sidetracked my modern mind, until I joined back in with Grandpa. "Thy will be done on earth as it is in heaven. Give us this day our daily bread and forgive us our trespasses as we forgive those who have trespassed against us. And lead us not into temptation, but deliver us from evil… For thine is the Kingdom and the power, and the glory forever and ever. Amen and Amen."

As Grandpa sat down, he was deeply disappointed by his forgotten prayer. But I was proud. I could see the sadness in his face, and I hoped that he could see the respect in my eyes. To those of us who loved him, each prayer seemed to rank up there with some of the most beautiful offered under the canopy of heaven by mortal man. It appeared as though Grandpa just prayed heaven down to earth, and for a moment the two met.

An "all-American" football player who was going to be sharing his testimony that morning, leaned over and whispered, "One of these days the Lord's going to call your grandpa for off-sides in prayers. He jumps in and out of prayers so fast he draws everyone 'off-sides.' The people are constantly closing their eyes and opening them, wondering if he's talking or praying."

The pastor on my other side whispered to me. "The older your grandpa gets, the more his talking and praying gets mixed up.

One of these days he's going to go into one long prayer and we'll have to pray along with him just to talk to him." All three of us chuckled.

My mind flashed back to a poem Grandpa loved to use when we would work on funerals together. The poem is at Idaho University on the base of the war memorial flagstaff. I was praying these words under my breath:

> *They shall not grow old,*
> *Age shall not weary them,*
> *Nor the years condemn,*
> *At the going down of the sun,*
> *And in the morning*
> *We shall remember them.*

CHAPTER TWO

A Cold River Called Loneliness

Let's look at the age of our grandparents

1890 The Sioux battle of "Wounded Knee."

1895 June 15th Emporia, Kansas *Gazette* notes old-fashioned "mover wagons," coming through town as homesteaders begin to give up 160 acre farms to move on and look for a place to begin again.

1900 US population 75,994,575; foreign born 10,341,276. Automobiles one for every 9,500 persons; 144 miles of hard surface roads in the country.

1903 August 1, first successful transcontinental automobile trip completed from San Francisco to New York, began May 23.

Geronimo, famous Apache leader, dies
FEBRUARY 17, 1909

He became a celebrity after appearing at the St. Louis World's Fair, but he will be best remembered as a symbol of the American Indian. Geronimo, leader of the Chiricahua Apaches, escaped from captivity four times before settling down to become a rancher. Before he died today at age 80, Geronimo said: "I was living peacefully with my family perfectly contented. Now there are very few of us left."

*Chronicle of the 20th Century, Chronicle Publications
Mount Kisco, New York, 1987, page 121*

eA Cold River Called Loneliness

*"These thoughts did make him stagger in his purposes,
but his follies prevailing more than any other reason,
he purposed to cause himself to be knighted."*

CERVANTES, *The Ingenious Gentleman
Don Quixote De La Mancha*

The visitor from another century was born in the nineteenth century, and when the twentieth century arrived he was alone. The twentieth century was brand new and many glorious adventures were taking place around the world when a lone, 10-year-old child walked the cold, windy streets of Boise, Idaho. After a time of wandering, Ephraim Goode found the main street. The clamor of the "Model A" on the road put fear in everyone within earshot, but for the 10-year-old it was terrifying. To combat the fear the boy tried to talk tough to himself. "I am a man and I can make it on my own." The tiny, red-headed boy with a strong chin and eyes of despair couldn't quite convince himself.

His hands were callused from bitter hard work. His face looked boyish by contrast to the sadness in his demeanor and the cold look in his eyes. The light of innocence and hope of childhood had long since gone out in those bluish-gray eyes.

Ephraim began to walk with a stride that said he knew where he was going. The last thing he wanted was for someone to discover how desperate he really felt. The cold mountain breeze began to whistle through the streets, and he fought his hunger by thinking over and over, "I'm a man and I don't need anyone!" As he walked, he glanced to his side and there it was — what he feared more than anything else in the world, the image of his own reflection in the shop window. As he looked into the reflection, his false confidence was shattered by real self-pity. He tried to push the thought out of his head, but it was too late.

"I'm no man — I'm just a child. And nobody cares." That thought ripped his heart. A flood of icy loneliness poured through the gaping hole into his soul. His weak legs sat down on the steps as he was lost in the rampaging current of killer thoughts. "I was never meant to be…. There is no place for me in this world." One after another, the cold current pounded him against such jagged rocks. His spirit was bruised irreparably as he surrendered to the mercy of the interminable current, which surged like it would drown his conscience, his hope, his determination — him. The cold north wind numbing his face felt warm by comparison to this deluge of self-pity. The little boy cried, or maybe it was his first prayer.

At that moment Ephraim heard laughter. It was like a lifeline for his sanity. He walked toward it desperately. He smelled food and ran after it uncontrollably. Looking into the diner, he settled himself and formulated a plan from his tortured despondency. He walked to the water pump to wash his face and hands. Glancing around to see if anyone was looking, he dusted off his clothes and tucked in his shirt. With confidence born from his distress, he walked into the cafe like a son of the leisure class and ordered dinner. All his life he would remember that meal. Never had food tasted so good! As he completed his feast, the proprietor came out from the kitchen. To Ephraim he looked like a rocky mountain grizzly. The bearded man growled, "Do you have money for that, kid?" "No sir, I ain't got it, but I be a hard worker." The boy's Ozark accent hinted at the drama of the first 10 years of his life.

Anger flashed in the eyes of the betrayed diner cook. "Why, you bastard! What do you think I am?" Rage immediately filled the boy with its burning poison. A storm of deep emotion passed through the boy's eyes and his face changed countenance, betraying the berserk fit about to erupt. "I ain't, I ain't!"

The big man held the screaming, hysterical boy at arms' length. "Okay, boy. Okay, boy. Okay! A boy your age shouldn't even know what that means...and no child on earth should have that hard look in their eyes! I can't afford a boy right now, but you can work for a few days until you find someone who can."

Ephraim waited tables and did dishes for his meals. And the man was good to him. Ephraim would always love to tell the story of the free meal throughout his life to illustrate the fact that you never know when you are going to run into a kind person.

He slept in the shed and felt pretty good except for the cold current of loneliness that would slip into his heart every night. Years later he would say with deep emotion, "No one deserves to feel that lonely! Everybody in the world needs someone to care."

During the early days of the twentieth century many families moved to Idaho to work on the railroad, for those were hard days. The expected work never came, and as a result many a family went without. Ephraim had journeyed from Arkansas with his family to find themselves in the same predicament. His family hadn't been in Idaho long before he felt he had to leave and make it on his own. According to his recollection, it was as much his fault that he had to leave as anything. He was, in his own words, "a wild, uncontrollable brat of a boy."

Asking around town for work, he came across a couple of men who suggested that he ask Dr. Collister, an old Irish surgeon, if he wanted to hire a boy. They had heard that he needed a low-priced laborer to work in his stables. The two men argued as they advised the boy. "What about what just happened? He won't want to see a boy. He'll want a man!"

Ephraim stepped in. "I am a man. Tell me how to get there!" Ephraim found the stables connected to a large apartment building near the Idaho State Capital. He asked in the apartments for Dr. Collister and was told that he was talking to a friend in front of the barn.

A power capsule inspired by Isaiah 61:1

The Spirit of the Sovereign Lord is on me, because the Lord has anointed me to preach good news to the poor. He has sent me to bind up the broken hearted, to proclaim freedom for the captives and release from darkness for the prisoners."

Never Underestimate God's Power to Repair and Restore!

As Ephraim came around the barn he saw two men. One was young, tall, and good-looking, with a kindly look on his face. Ephraim looked the man right in the eye and said, "Dr. Collister, I heer'd ya got work for a good man."

The man smiled warmly. "Don't look at me, that's Dr. Collister."

Ephraim trembled and stuttered out a half statement. "I bbbbbe..."

A venomous explosion of cursing erupted from the old Irish doctor. "...I'm not running an orphanage; I only have work for men!"

Ephraim looked him in the eye. "I be a man!"

Both of the men laughed and the laughter brought a little better feeling. "Okay, you've got to move this stack of 50-pound bags of coal up to the second floor. If you can't handle that then you can't work for me or anybody in this town," the doctor lectured defiantly. The two men walked off chuckling at the cocky kid.

Ephraim stepped inside the barn, closed the door, and grabbed a bag struggling to lift it. He grumbled, "I ain't much more'n 50 pounds." He hit that bag with a fury and managed to get it to the top after 10 minutes. He practically collapsed, thinking, "I cain't do this all day, I'll die." The river of self-pity began to flow again through its established channel. "It ain't no use, I just ain't meant to be."

After five minutes of feeling sorry for himself, he thought, "I got to get to work...I cain cry after'n I be fired and starved." Suddenly, that determined thought cleared his mind of self-pity and new creative ideas came into his head. He threw a rope over the rafter, tied one end to a horse and the other end to a sack of coal. About the time he had it all rigged up the two men came back.

Dr. Collister said, "I knew the little brat couldn't do it."

The younger man was a famous engineer in the state of Idaho and he interrupted. "Wait a minute, Doc, this isn't just a boy — he's an engineer. Look at this set-up. I'd hire him."

The doctor replied reluctantly, "Okay, you can sleep in the barn and I'll pay you whatever you deserve at the end of the day. But you have to earn your job every day. There will be plenty of chores to do just to be a part of the team and if you so much as blink I'll kick you out in the street on your butt!"

Several weeks later, Ephraim paid to have a letter sent. It was brief and to the point:

> *Mama,*
>
> *Ya should know it warn't anybody's fault I left. I didn't want to ruin your'n family...with hard times; this is what had to be.*
>
> *Love,*
>
> *Ephraim*

That night Ephraim dropped into his bed completely exhausted. He was sore and discouraged as he thought, "Every day gets worse." He went to sleep feeling the cold current of self-hatred, which had become his companion.

A prayer by Rev. Floyd White at age 85:

Our compassionate Father, we come to you with our burdens from the past, for we are sure, that in your matchless grace, you will make them lighter and grant us strength to bear them. Lord, make the difficulties and shadows that engulf us become the means to reveal to us the depth of your mercies. Our finite minds cannot grasp the significance of your plan of salvation, when you sent your son "to seek and save those that are lost." Amid the pains and hardships of life, we pray that you will comfort us by the warmth and power of your presence.

Amen and Amen.

CHAPTER THREE

Growing Up
Alone

A look at the day that is slowly being forgotten...

RUSSIA, APRIL 3, 1907
Twenty million people are starving in the
worst famine on record to date.

USA, AUGUST 12, 1908
Ford's first Model T is produced in Detroit —
"a motor car for the multitude."

LONDON, JANUARY 1, 1909
Astronomers sight what may be a planet
beyond Neptune. On the same day
Captain Robert Falcon Scott sets out
on a journey to conquer the South Pole.

MEXICO CITY, MAY 25, 1911
Pancho Villa overthrows Mexican President
Porfirio Diaz, who had been a virtual
dictator of Mexico since 1876.

WASHINGTON D.C., JUNE 12, 1911
US Senators to be elected directly by the
people instead of being voted
in by states' legislature.

Football deaths up

November 28, 1909

With the revelation that the death toll from football in 1909 had nearly doubled from the total for the previous year, the call was sounded anew for the reformation of the gridiron sport. Twenty-six players were killed and 70 seriously injured thus far this year, according to figures assembled by the *Chicago Tribune*. In 1907, there were 14 deaths and 13 in 1908. The rules committee is considering changes that would remove some of the perils of the sport, including one that would ban substitution of a player who has been ruled off the field for roughness.

Chronicle of the 20th Century, Chronicle Publications,
Mount Kisco, New York, 1987, page 130

Growing Up
Alone

"Don Quixote, Seeing himself in so ill plight, said to his squire, "Sancho I have heard say ofttimes, that to do good to men unthankful is to cast water into the sea."

CERVANTES, *The Ingenious Gentleman*
Don Quixote De La Mancha

"Oh no, not again at two o'clock in the morning," Ephraim muttered. But the bell kept ringing. There was an emergency at the Basque sheep camp. Ephraim awakened the doctor and hurried to start the car. The old Irish doctor came out to the car carrying his "little black bag." They were going to a large sheep ranch, and their course led northwest out of Boise, through the upper dry creek country, far out toward the mountains.

On the drive out to the sheep camp, Ephraim thought about his friendship with the doctor over the past few years. The Irish doctor's temper often flared and he cussed at the young man.

But Ephraim didn't mind, because he knew that deep down the old doctor really cared for him. Ephraim would tell people that the old doctor was the only man he ever met who could use filthy language and it didn't sound bad. The doctor was like the cactus that grew in the Snake River desert: he was prickly on the outside, but soft on the inside. There were many times when people couldn't pay him, but he would help them anyway. During the past few years, Ephraim had learned manners and good grammar, and had the opportunity to go to school. The doctor had been good to Ephraim.

This Irish surgeon was born in Willoughley, Ohio, in 1856. He attended the state university and Heron Medical College in Cleveland. Soon after graduation, he had moved to Boise, where his sister lived. She was the wife of Judge Huston, who served on the State Supreme Court.

The doctor was a leader in working with germ theory as well as research on Rocky Mountain spotted fever. Dr. and Mrs. Collister had become quite wealthy through the years. They owned a large farm, extensive peach orchards, and a dairy herd. They also owned a big cattle ranch on Soldier Creek above Emmett, Idaho. Add to that their apartments, real estate holdings, and another cattle ranch, and the total equaled quite a sizeable estate for that day. The old doctor and the redheaded boy from the Ozarks were from two different worlds, and Ephraim was curious about the doctor's friendship with him.

When they arrived at the sheep ranch, Ephraim settled down in the back seat of the car for a good nap. The doctor had gone inside to assist with the miracle of another birth. Blissful sleep was beginning to engulf Ephraim, when a loud voice penetrated his dreams. "We're having trouble in there, Ephraim, and you have to help me." The doctor's voice was rough with tension. He had asked for help before, and had more or less prepared Ephraim to assist in emergencies. This was a desperate situation, as there was no time to take the patient to the hospital, which was some 25 miles away over rough roads. In those pre-dawn hours, Ephraim witnessed something he never forgot...a determined and compassionate physician performing a skillful act of his profession. At sun-up, a strong, lusty Basque baby and mother were resting peacefully.

As he returned to the car, Ephraim was all but falling asleep on his feet. The old doctor was tired and grumpy, and looking forward to a nap on the way home. Ephraim sat at the wheel as the tired doctor returned to the shanty for one last load. When the doctor returned, he stretched out in the back seat of the car and said, "Let's go home, son." The car sputtered, remaining in its place. "Ephraim, let's go, damn it," growled the doctor. There was still no sound. The doctor shook Ephraim awake. "Never mind, I'll drive. You get in the back, you goddamn bastard. What do you think I pay you for?" Immediately, Ephraim turned red with rage, saying nothing as he moved to the backseat. The doctor had never seen Ephraim act in this way. He turned around to get another look. Ephraim had tears rolling down his cheeks. He was staring out the window with a long empty look, like he had just lost everything that mattered to him. In point of fact, the cold river of loneliness and self-hate was simply running its familiar course again.

When they finally reached home, the doctor shook Ephraim awake. "Ephraim, tomorrow, I mean today, you start eating your meals with the wife, daughter, and myself." Ephraim smiled as he heard those words. Ephraim started to walk away, but the doctor called out, "Ephraim...I...I. You know I'm just a crusty old Irishman, don't you?" Ephraim nodded his head and replied, "That's all right, Doc. It's me. I irritate people. I always have. If you want me to leave, just give me the word."

The doctor's eyes softened. "It's not you, Ephraim. I never wanted to see another boy again...I just wasn't ready...I guess I'll never be ready. It's an ache inside my chest that never goes away. It's an anger, and there is nothing I can do about it."

Ephraim grabbed at the bait. "What are you always so mad about, Doc?"

The doctor drew a breath before he replied. "I'm mad about life, and how unfair it is. I'm mad at God, if He's up there!" The doctor forced the words out slowly. "Mrs. Collister and I had a son...he was our own child. There were so many good times...the first time I held him and introduced myself to him, and then introduced him to the world! The first time he walked, I felt so proud! I can still see him taking those steps with his hands in the air, thinking I was holding on. And the nights that he would come and get in bed with us after he had a nightmare. When I would come home, he would come running and call me 'Daddy!' He used to love to help me work on any project. Since the time he was just a little runt, we would go hunting together every fall. We would ride together, fish together. He was so intelligent...so handsome. When he was a teenager he fell in love and it made me feel good inside." The doctor stopped talking. He simply couldn't say anymore.

Ephraim said, "Doc, you don't have to tell me this."

"Yes, I do," said the man who was old enough to be his grandfather. "He was killed in a hunting accident. Part of me died that day and that part hurts when I'm around you. I want you to leave, Ephraim, but I would die if you did."

Ephraim broke in, "Doggone it, Doc, don't put that on me, I'm just a worthless nobody. You and Mrs. Collister don't mean anything to me. You're just an old couple that I conned a job and a bed from. Don't be any more stupid than you have to be."

The doctor straightened his back. "You're right, I'm just a crusty, hot-headed Irishman, and you are just a beggar who thinks he's a man." As Ephraim walked toward his sleeping quarters, the doctor called out, "I still want you to eat with us. We can talk over your work better that way. I've got to do something to get my money's worth from a no-good beggar like you!"

When Ephraim moved into the house with the Collisters, he knew that their daughter Edna was going to be a problem. They were both teenagers at Boise High School. Ephraim was popular. In fact, he would become the Student Body President his senior year. That isn't to say that he didn't have his wild side, because he did. But in no way did it compare to the wild side of Edna Collister.

At first, Edna was constantly flirting with Ephraim. Their relationship developed into one where they vacillated between attraction and hatred, and these extremes would continue to grow more pronounced. Their relationship slowly turned into sibling rivalry as they competed for everything. Bickering turned into bitterness, and bitterness developed into cold, silent hate.

One night at the dinner table, Ephraim revealed a lie that Edna was telling about something she had done at school. Her eyes shot daggers at Ephraim. As she buttered her cornbread she said sweetly, "Ephraim, who are we supposed to believe? You aren't even a Collister; you are just a bastard!"

Before Ephraim knew what was taking place, he was going berserk. He stood up and slapped Edna so hard that it made her nose bleed. Dr. Collister immediately grabbed Ephraim and threw him up against the wall, cracking his head against a shelf. When Ephraim stopped struggling, the doctor yelled, "Get out of here! Who do you think you are, anyway?"

Ephraim went to his room and started to pack his belongings. Outside the door he heard Mary Collister tell her husband, "He's just a boy. Go talk to him, please, for me?" As the doctor entered Ephraim's room, Ephraim tried to hide his tears. "What came over you?" the doctor asked.

Ephraim put on his tough facade and continued packing. "You guys don't mean anything to me. I don't need anyone. I'm a man, and I can make it on my own. It's time for me to leave."

The doctor said in a stronger voice, "I didn't ask what time it was. I asked what came over you!"

Ephraim dodged his question. "I don't know; it's just time for me to leave."

A power capsule
inspired by 2 Corinthians 5:16

So from now on we regard no one from a worldly point of view. Though we once regarded Christ in this way, we do so no longer.

No one can make you feel inferior without your consent!

The doctor grabbed him again, showing surprising strength. "You're not leaving until you tell me what came over you."

"All right," Ephraim cried. "She was right, I am a bastard. I should have never been born." Tears streamed down his cheeks, and he began to let out uncontrollable sighs. His face turned red from embarrassment. He was too old to let anyone see him bawl. "I don't know who I am, or if there is any reason for my miserable life. White, the last name that I have been using, isn't really my name. I hate the name Ephraim. I'm a nobody!"

The doctor let go of Ephraim, saying, "I'm sorry."

"So am I," said Ephraim. "Everyone is sorry. The Texan named Goode that got my mama pregnant was sorry, too."

The doctor looked as though he were in surgery, and did not know what to do. "I don't know what to say, except that you are welcome to stay on here — we won't use that word against you anymore. Maybe together, we'll somehow find out who we both are," the doctor said kindly.

Ephraim acted like he had to leave. He threw his things in a bag. The doctor spoke more anxiously. "Ephraim, you're a good worker, you know that. We're not doing you a favor; you would be doing us a favor. I need all the help I can get on the ranch. I was hoping to start breaking you in as a ranch hand. Shoot, maybe someday you'll be my foreman. A trusted fore-man is hard to find. It would take a great load off my shoul-ders." The doctor left the room, hoping to find Ephraim there the next day.

The next day at school, Edna confronted Ephraim. She had an ambitious power about her, and she was brief and to the point. "He may treat you like a son, but I'll make sure you'll never get a son's inheritance!" It was stubbornness and hatred for Edna that made Ephraim return to the Collisters with every inten-tion of staying.

Several months later, another night call came in the midst of a storm. This time they had to journey to Atlanta, Idaho, to help a miner who was very ill. Ephraim checked the car and made sure they had plenty of gas. He also put in chains, an axe, and shovels, because a severe storm was predicted for the mountain regions.

It was raining when they left Boise, but by the time they reached Featherville the rain had changed to snow. By the time they came to Rock Creek, the headlights revealed that the pole bridge had washed out in the rushing torrent. Ephraim started to turn the car around. "What in the world do you think you are doing?" exclaimed the doctor.

"What else can we do? There isn't a way," answered Ephraim.

"We'll find a way," replied the doctor.

Working together, they cut down the banks of the river and filled in the stream with brush and rocks. The mixture of snow, rain, and hail pounded fiercely down upon them, reminding them of nature's violent power. As the car plunged down into the turbulent stream, Ephraim let out a panicked yell, "This is stupid! We could die! Nobody expects us to try this hard!"

As the car motored across the river, the doctor said calmly, "It's not what other people expect, it's what I expect!" This pattern was repeated at several washouts. As they plunged into the turbulent stream at each crossing, they wondered if they could make it any further. Ephraim was wondering just how far the doctor would go. After eight hours of hazardous driving in the sleet and snow, they arrived at the mining camp and were directed to a little building near the cook shack, where they found the patient in critical condition.

The doctor's examination revealed that the patient could not survive the trip to a hospital, and that he would die if they did not operate. The only alternative was to operate at the camp. The doctor had surmised that this might be necessary and had brought along his surgical instruments. A table was made ready in the mess hall, and the cook brought a big pile of clean dishtowels, as there were no sheets in the camp. Two of the miners were drafted to help prepare the man for the operation, and two others cleaned and filled all the available lanterns. They hung them from the ceiling over the makeshift operating table.

Ephraim's job was to sterilize the surgical instruments in a wash boiler on the wood stove. The patient was strapped to the table with ropes, and Ephraim was given instructions for administering the anesthetic. He stood at Dr. Collister's side, holding the instruments on a large meat platter, and occasionally mopping sweat from the doctor's forehead.

Finally, the operation was completed and the exhausted surgeon gave directions for the patient's care to the miner who had been appointed as nurse. As they left, the doctor remarked that the man only had a fifty-fifty chance. Dr. Collister told Ephraim, "It's up to the Almighty now!"

About a month or so later, as Ephraim was picking up the doctor from his Boise office, he saw the same miner being ushered in. "Hello, Doc! You fellas don't remember me, do you?" the miner said with a grin. "I'm the guy you carved on that night in the cook shack. I'm sound as a dollar now, and I've come to thank you for saving my life. The fellers told me about your trip on that stormy night, and the operation by lantern light. You saved my life! Here, this ought to more than cover what I owe ya." The miner handed the doctor a sack of gold dust. "Part of this is for that young feller who helped you."

Ephraim protested, "I'm no doctor. I didn't do anything." The miner looked right at him with a grin only a gold miner could have. The twinkle in his eye was fueled from lost mines yet to be discovered. To emphasize this remark, he pointed his grubby finger right at him, and Ephraim had never seen a hand so beat-up. The miner raised his voice as though he was preparing for a fight in a saloon.

"Listen here, kid, and never forget it! That night you believed that you were a doctor, and it was good enough to help save my life. *In these here United States of America, it's not who you are, but what you believe that counts!* Take the gold."

That single encounter was to have a lasting effect on Ephraim. The romantic idealism of the gold miner inspired him to fantasize of being a gold miner, and may have played a part in his life-long hobby as a rock hound.

Doctor Collister took the gold and exchanged it for currency. Those three new 10-dollar bills certainly looked good to Ephraim. Ephraim had thought a lot about what the miner had said, so he went to talk to Dr. Collister about it. He asked how he could legally change his name. The doctor told him, "One of these days, Mrs. Collister and I may want to legally adopt you and Edna." Ephraim looked like a double-barreled shotgun had hit him. "But, but I thought Edna's name was Collister?" he said sheepishly.

"No," said the doctor. "Her real name is Edna Simpson. Her mother died as I was delivering Edna, and we've raised her. Our son was Mrs. Collister's and my only child." Although Edna did not know that Ephraim knew her secret, their relationship continued to become increasingly distant and antagonistic.

After much thought, Ephraim went to the courthouse and legally changed his name to Floyd Edward White. Edward White was the name of his stepfather, and he had always been good to Ephraim. In fact, there were times when Edward White even worked for the Collisters. The main reason that Ephraim had left the White family in the first place was because of his temper and his struggle for identity. This led to terrible bouts of self-pity. He knew that if he was going to change his name, this was one name that would make his mamma proud.

With his new name, Floyd walked down the same street he had walked as a 10-year-old. He thought about his real mother, his stepfather, his real brother and sisters, and how he cared deeply for each of them. He reflected upon the Collisters and his deep feelings for them. Now as he looked in a window and saw his reflection, instead of self-pity came pride. He said out loud, "Floyd Edward White! Now that is a name that I choose! The twentieth century is young and *in these United States of America it's not who you are, but what you believe that counts!"*

The Collisters readily accepted Floyd's name change. However, when he was alone with Edna, she called him Ephraim, and let him know that one way or another, she would see him turned into the streets with nothing from the Collisters.

To avoid further conflict, the Collisters had Floyd go to work for the summer at the ranch on Soldier Creek above Emmett, Idaho. They reasoned that the life of a cowboy would be tough, but it would certainly build his character.

A prayer by Rev. Floyd E. White after writing a devotional about Dr. Collister:

Thank you, Dear Father, for Christ, the Great Physician, whose touch can make us whole. We thank you for the kind, concerned people that help others over difficult places in life. Open our eyes that we may acquire something of their selfless love for the needy, the hurting, and the unlovely. Give us courage and faith to venture forth wherever you lead. Help us, our Heavenly Father, to take more time to discover the richness of your Word, and the time to understand the Love that motivates those who have dedicated their lives to helping others. In the Perfect name of Christ we pray.

Amen and Amen.

CHAPTER FOUR

I Will Lift Mine Eyes Unto the Hills

Remington has depicted his last cowboy

DECEMBER 26, 1909

Sculptor and painter Frederic Remington died this morning at age 48 when an acute case of appendicitis was not treated in time.

Remington once said, "I knew more about cowboys than I did about drawing." He was, in fact, an expert on both. Born in upper New York State, he studied art at Yale. Restless after college, he got work as a cow-herder out West. At six feet tall with broad shoulders, he fared as well as any ranch hand.

Remington's first Western-influenced painting was commissioned by *Harper's Weekly* in the early 1880s. It depicted a scene from Geronimo's campaign. Later, the artist illustrated Theodore Roosevelt's series of cowboy articles. Remington also worked deftly in bronze; "The Bucking Bronco" may be his finest sculpture.

Chronicle of the 20th Century, Chronicle Publications, Mount Kisco, New York, 1987, page 131

Popular Mark Twain mourned in America

APRIL 21, 1910

Several years ago, a newspaper erroneously ran an article announcing Mark Twain's demise. Twain saw the article and swiftly corrected the paper. "The reports of my death," he wrote, "are greatly exaggerated." Today, the passing is real. Samuel Langhorne Clemens, America's eminent author and humorists, is dead at 74.

Chronicle of the 20th Century, Chronicle Publications,
Mount Kisco, New York, 1987, page 137

I Will Lift Mine Eyes Unto the Hills

"So great is mine affection," replied Don Quixote, *"to serve you, as I was fully resolved never to depart out of these mountains until I had found you, and known of yourself whether there might be ant remedy for your grief."*

CERVANTES, *The Ingenious Gentleman Don Quixote De La Mancha*

"Roll out! Come a runnin'!" The clanging of the iron spoon on the iron pot was the first noise heard over the distant roar of the spring run-off from Soldier Creek. Floyd stuck his head out of his bedroll to see only the blackness of mountain night. "Roll out! Come a runnin'," came the call of the Cookie.

Floyd stuck his head back under his bedroll and groaned, "Call me when it's light." The young ranch hand next to him groaned, "Only a fool argues with a skunk, a mule or a cook." They both slipped their boots on, noticing that frost had covered everything. The old cowboy next to them said, "You young bucket doggies don't know what the life of a cowboy is all about. Before barbed wire we lived out here most of the time. Kickin' never gets you nowhere lessn' your'n a mule. Get up and get some grub — it's gonna be a long day."

The dozen men rolled and tied their beds and ate breakfast quickly. By then the wranglers had brought the horses in at a run. The men chose the ones they wanted and saddled up. The roundup captain yelled out, "Fan out, and bring in everything with hair and horns!" By ones, by bunches, the cattle were rounded up and headed toward the roundup ground.

Floyd did the best he could, but by seven o'clock he'd accomplished nothing. The grass was still white with the night's frost and a light fog was rising from the ground. To the east the sun was a dull yellow ball at the gray horizon. The towering Sawtooth Mountains still appeared as a distant shadow. Floyd thought, "This has been my dream for a long time — now if I can just figure out what in the heck I'm doing." The roundup captain found Floyd in the middle of a meadow watching a mule deer bound away. "Just stick with me kid — ya gotta get trained for this, or you could get hurt." Floyd protested, "But I'm a good worker!" The foreman kept riding as he said, "Listen kid, out here my word's law…doesn't matter if the doc owns everything, I'm the law and you do what I say. Besides, tossin' your rope before mak'n a loop don't catch the calf."

Noon saw over 100 head gathered into one herd, milling about in a cloud of dust. The yellow blossoms of the sagebrush were highlighted by the distant white snowcaps.

Some men continued combing the hills for strays while others set about "cutting" the herd, separating it into smaller herds.

For this work, the cowboys rode their cutting horses, which were the most agile and highly trained.

When one cowboy grabbed a cow and her calf from the herd, another roped the calf and dragged it to the fire where the branding irons were heated. After wrestling the struggling calf to the ground, the calf was held by two men while a third drew the red-hot branding iron from the fire and pressed it quickly and carefully to the calf's side. The calf bawled. Other calves bawled. Cows bawled. For the next several years that sound would become Floyd's constant companion. A cowboy gets used to it, and he feels lonely without it. Those cattle never shut up!

Later he would say that being a cowboy is no different from being a pastor. Only the people don't have horns — or at least most of them.

One man's job was to earmark each calf, using a sharp knife to cut the ear. Most of the bull calves were castrated at branding time to change them to steers. Steers were easier to handle and better for beef. Only the best calves were kept as bulls for breeding.

The branding, earmarking, and castrating of a calf took only a minute or two. Then the men started on the next one. All afternoon the work went on hot and heavy, with the churned up dust rising in clouds and mixing with the smoke from the fire and the odors of sweat and burning hair. While the men were displaying their skill with the cattle, Floyd was fixing fence line and digging up poisonous plants. By the time it was dark, Floyd felt like he would drop. He rode to the camp and prepared his bed when he received a strong kick in the pants that sent him tumbling. "A cowboy's not done till he takes care of his horse. Next time you are fired!" The roundup captain turned back to the mess line. After taking care of his horse, Floyd grabbed dinner and hit the sack. It would all begin again at 3:00 a.m.

Later in his life his grandchildren used to laugh at Floyd because he wouldn't go to bed on a cold night without going out and covering his car with a blanket. And after they returned from a vacation he would spot his car still at home and cry out with joy, "Well, look at that good old boy — he's still waiting in the driveway for us." It was as if he expected his car to be out running through the fields when he was gone.

After the spring roundup, life wasn't much easier for Floyd. He was responsible for feeding and milking the cows, taking care of the pasture, building sheds, and cleaning the barns. Floyd thought this was child's work. He decided he would prove his skill by breaking his saddle horse. That was his first mistake. Stubbornness is an attribute for a cowboy, but it can kill a person while he is learning. He used the same tactics that he had learned from watching the seasoned cowboys. He spent all his spare time in working with a wild mare. The other ranchhands told him that she was kept only as a brood mare, and she was also too old to break for riding.

Floyd's stubbornness seemed to win out. In the process he earned his share of spills with all the resulting bruises and scratches. Soon he had gentled her and could ride her for some distance without much trouble. With the arrogance of youth, he felt that he had really shown the others that he knew something about horses.

On a hot August day, as the men were out attempting to hold the cattle to the higher ranges, Floyd decided to put his newly trained horse to work. He had neglected to take salt up to a certain canyon for sometime, and this would be a good opportunity. Since Floyd was rushed, he did not take time to change into his boots and chaps, but instead wore the light pair of shoes he had been wearing while working around the ranch house. As he rode out of the corral, the mare took off in her characteristic canter. Floyd was elated as he breezed along. He felt that he had never experienced such a smooth ride.

Just at the height of this feeling of exhilaration, he realized that the trail suddenly began to climb, and a short distance ahead there was a sharp curve. The mare had struck her gait and did not heed his attempts to rein her under control. The more he pulled on the reins and talked to her, the more excited she became, until she was running up the steep trail at an alarming pace. It was then that he saw the washout on the curve. He was unable to avoid it as the mountain rose perpendicular on one side, with the canyon threatening on the other side. The mare was now wildly excited as she attempted to jump the wash. She lost her footing and over she went, rolling down the draw and carrying Floyd with her. Amazingly, she landed on her feet, but Floyd was underneath her as the saddle had turned on her body and his shoe was caught in the stirrup. The terrorized horse started to run, dragging Floyd with her. Floyd remembered stories about men being dragged to death, as he bounced back and forth under the crazed animal. He grabbed at bushes and rocks, thinking that his time had come. He could feel those hooves as they fanned his face. He realized that if he had worn his heavy chaps, he would not have torn up his skin. Or for that matter, if he had worn his boots, his shoe would not have caught in the stirrup.

After minutes of the most grueling experience a man could endure, his shoestring broke. He pulled his way free from the stirrup, and the frightened horse continued down the canyon.

Floyd lay still for sometime to clear his head. He began to compare his life to that experience. He knew well the emotional feeling of being dragged without control. The one difference was that physical pain hurt less than emotional pain. He climbed up as he looked to the massive snow-capped mountains. The view stirred something deeply inside him, and the hair on the back of his neck stood up. Under his breath he thanked the Almighty for a broken shoestring.

After getting up, he found he had not broken any bones. His clothes were in shreds, and he had many bruises to help him remember this lesson. His hands and face were the worst. He began to remove some stickers and gravel as he limped down the trail. After sometime, he saw a ranch hand coming after him. The veteran cowboy had become worried when he saw the frightened mare in the corral, and had put two and two together. As Floyd jumped on the back of the ranch-hand's horse, the old cowboy mumbled, "Just because your pants have polished a saddle, it don't make you a rider."

After hearing about that experience, the doctor gave orders that Floyd should be given the best cattle pony that they could find, and an experienced white-gray horse named Old Cap fit the bill. Although Old Cap wasn't a purebred, he had developed a reputation in the Snake River country as a top cutting horse. This old horse literally taught Floyd how to be a cowboy. Old Cap knew just how to set his feet when a steer had been roped. That was an essential technique, and if performed wrongly could cost both the horse and rider their lives. There wasn't a bull in Idaho that could intimidate Old Cap. He could climb hills that would put fear in another horse, and he seemed to have a sixth sense in the dark.

For a young man growing up alone, the very best part of being a cowboy was the companionship that he felt with his horse.

Through the years of working his way up to foreman, Floyd had ridden many horses. But he loved Old Cap like he had never loved anything before.

Old Cap seemed to understand everything Floyd said, or even felt. As an old man, Floyd loved an amazing number of people, yet he always said that Old Cap was probably the best friend he ever had. In fact, he believed this horse was smarter than 90 percent of the people he had met, and that statement was not meant as a put-down against humanity.

Old Cap saved Floyd's life several times. The first winter after Floyd had graduated from high school, a terrible blizzard hit the high country. The Collisters had moved to the ranch house after Floyd and Edna graduated. The rest of the ranch hands were out gathering strays as Floyd finished supper, and he prepared Old Cap to join them. Mrs. Collister had a funny feeling about this trip, and the howling sounds of the storm pushed her to insist that Floyd would stay and work in the barn. Floyd kept on getting Old Cap ready; as he said, "I'm a man; I'll do a man's work." Mrs. Collister insisted, "The other men left before the storm, but if they were here now they would stay." Dr. Collister interceded for him, and Floyd headed out to the high country on Old Cap.

The storm became worse as the night grew late, and all the men returned — except Floyd. The doctor and a couple of the veteran ranch hands saddled up fresh mounts and headed out to look for Floyd. Visibility was practically impossible. Mrs. Collister screamed at the doctor, "Find him, because I can't live through losing another son!" The foreman replied, "Ma'am, if anyone can bring him back, Old Cap can."

Mrs. Collister was praying by the fire when she heard the men return. It wasn't too long before her husband entered and told her, "It's no use, Mary. There is just too much storm to risk more lives." Mrs. Collister kept praying. Later that night, her prayers were interrupted by the familiar whinny of Old Cap. By the time she ran outside, the ranch hands were pulling Floyd off Old Cap and carrying him to the house. Evidently, he had been severely injured by a bull and had climbed back on Old Cap before passing out. Old Cap brought him home safely through one of the worst winters in Idaho's history.

After Mrs. Collister and the doctor had taken care of Floyd, she put on her wraps and walked to the barn in the middle of the night. She lit the lantern and fed some sugar to Old Cap. With tears in her eyes, she hugged the old horse and cried, "Thank you."

Those days of working next to the towering Sawtooth Mountains began to have an impact on Floyd. Sometimes as he mended fence lines, he would stop and listen to the chipmunks and just soak up the message of the indomitable mountains. On other occasions, he would ride Old Cap up Soldier Creek. This land was so big and rugged, and the green pines and aspens turning yellow from the first frost were arranged in beautiful colors. More than once, Floyd would get off Old Cap and lay by the stream, dunking his head in a deep green-blue pool. He drank the fresh mountain water with open eyes as he watched the trout. At such times, Floyd suspected that there was an Almighty Creator.

Floyd was not a saint. He had many of the vices for which ranch hands are famous. During those cowboy days, Floyd made mistakes that he never felt he had to share with others later in his life. Floyd's temper continued to get him into as much trouble as any young man could handle.

Once, when he and the doctor were in Boise, the doctor saw him eyeing a woman with a terrible reputation. The doctor warned him to stay away from the lady, who was twice Floyd's age. The doctor got his "Irish up" and that pushed Floyd to do just what he was told not to do: Floyd joined the woman in her room for a bottle of liquor. He knew that trouble always accompanied drink for him, but he did not care. He was heavily under the influence when a knock came at the door of the lady's room. It was Mrs. Collister. Floyd jumped out of the window and started running. He had been fully clothed in the room, but as he ran he became so hot that he began shedding his clothes, making a bad situation worse. Finally, Dr. Collister caught him. The doctor ended the incident by calling Floyd names that only he was allowed to call him, and Floyd went into a depression that lasted for several weeks.

At the urging of Mrs. Collister, the doctor approached Floyd to see if there was something wrong. They had never seen him so depressed. The doctor explained to him that they were very disappointed in him again. They were proud of his work, but it was time that he pulled his life together. He looked right in Floyd's eyes when he said, "It is just that Mrs. Collister and I trust you and Edna with so much." Floyd turned away as if those words hurt. The doctor continued, "I know that I cuss you out worse than anyone has a right to, and most of the time I treat you like a ranch hand. But I never believed that I could have loved another boy. That is, until you started to get under my skin. In fact, someday, Floyd, I'm leaving the Soldier Creek ranch to you. You deserve it!"

"But what about Edna?" the young man queried.

The old doctor continued, "I've decided that we will legally adopt you and Edna only when you develop a determination and commitment to help people. Besides, there are two ranches and she can have one."

The next day, the doctor inquired again about Floyd's continuing blue mood. "Floyd, didn't you hear me right yesterday? When I'm gone you'll be rich. I'm going to leave you a fortune, you deserve it."

"It is not that," Floyd said slowly. "You said that you were disappointed with me. I'm disappointed with me; I'm disappointed with my whole life. I've always had this feeling like I am a mistake. I don't know why I'm even alive, or if life is even worth living. Life is hell, I want to die. Maybe I've gone crazy, Doc."

A power capsule inspired by Romans 12:2

"Do not conform any longer to the pattern of this world, but be transformed by the renewing of your mind. Then you will be able to test and approve what God's will is, his good, pleasing and perfect will."

Change Your Ideas and You Can Change Your World!

"Whatever is true, whatever is noble, whatever is right, whatever is pure, whatever is lovely, whatever is admirable — if anything is excellent or praiseworthy — think about such things."

A couple of days later, Dr. Collister stepped into the bunkhouse. "Floyd, would you like to see a man hung? I'm the supervising doctor at an execution in Boise. Would you like to go?"

"You bet," the young man replied excitedly.

It was an icy cold day in Boise. The doctor and Floyd stood below the scaffolding as the condemned man was brought out. The crowd was large and the atmosphere seemed like a carnival. Floyd felt the excitement in the air as he thought about how lucky he was to have such an important place to stand. The wind whipped his hair wildly as he held onto the doctor's bag and the doctor held onto his hat. Floyd noticed other spectators looking enviously at their spot for the hanging. The state officials maintained their official demeanor as the cursing, condemned man stepped up to have the rope put around his neck. The convict spat at the crowd and struggled against the guards. The profanity spewing from his mouth was revolting to Floyd, although his own vocabulary wasn't exactly Sunday school proper itself. The look of the man was evil in every way. Floyd thought to himself, "If anyone deserves to die, this man does." The appointed individual turned on the water which would ultimately fill the bucket and pull the latch, so that no one would feel guilty for the murder. One spectator commented to another about the advance of science in the twentieth century to invent such a thing. The suspense was incredible. Suddenly, the crowd began to cheer, which was followed by a ghostly silence. The bucket was frozen, and the device would not work. The condemned victim continued to curse the crowd as he laughed a long, perverted laugh. It sounded as if he had just gotten away with a crime. His tough demeanor began to turn into a frantic, crazed stream of profanity. The state representatives brought out hot water and poured it over the ice to free up the mechanism.

Bang! The trap door flung open as this human being fell, breaking his neck as designed. His open eyes seemed to bulge and look right through Floyd, even though there was a black sack about his head. And then deep, almost from his soul, came a low moan of anguish, "Ahhhhhh…. Ohhhhh…" as if death had confronted him with the misery of his wasted life. The legs began to kick nervously, and the smell of human feces filled the air. Floyd stared as the doctor felt the body for a pulse, then nodded to the officials.

All his life, Floyd was determined that capital punishment was wrong. He would later argue with his grandson, "If you've witnessed one, you would feel the same way."

On the way back, Floyd kept hearing that moan of a wasted life. He couldn't get the picture of that man's look or the smell out of his mind. The moan grew in his mind. *Ahhhhhhhhhh. Ohhhhhhhhhhh.* Finally he cried out, "Stop the car, Doc!" He jumped out and ran down the hill by the creek, and leaned against a big Ponderosa Pine. The vomiting became uncontrollable. His head began to spin as he kept hearing that moan until he passed out, falling into his vomit.

The next thing he knew, the doctor was washing off his face with cold water as his head rested on an exposed root of the mighty Ponderosa. The cold breeze felt good now, but it seemed to call his name, and he deeply sensed that there was a plan for his life.

The doctor spoke softly, more tenderly than Floyd had heard recently. It was as if he were easing a distressed Basque mother as he was delivering a new baby. As Floyd looked at the doctor, it dawned on him that this powerful man was really pretty old. Because the doctor had such a strong presence, Floyd almost never thought of him in terms of age. But now wisdom shone from the old doctor's face.

"Life can be hell, Floyd. I was nine years old when the Civil War ended, but I can still remember seeing young men in love who were engaged to be married. They left for war, never to return. Young men who had left marching in glorious parades came back without arms or legs. But the worst was seeing young men after battle, because when you looked into their eyes, you could see that somehow they had lost their heart. What a tragedy."

The old man and the young man looked up to the majestic mountains. They noticed the deep green of the pine trees against the blue of the winter sky. The doctor sat on a massive granite rock made soft by the colonies of moss growing there. The air smelled so fresh, and the splashing sound of the creek soothed the soul.

The doctor continued, "I can still remember once near the end of the Civil War, we traveled near the sickening smell of death at a battlefield. That stench would sicken the countryside for miles, and it came from the bodies of young men shot down in the prime of life. Those young men were once little boys who sucked their thumbs. You know, I'm an educated man, but for the life of me, I still don't know why we had to fight that war. The issues were more important than most wars, but they could have been resolved without that!

"Life can be hell, Floyd. But it can be heaven, too. Life is precious. Life is fragile, it's short and it's so precious. There is nothing like falling in love, and not caring about anything else except being near the person you love; or children and their squeals, their hugs, the flicker in their eyes, or flowers. Flowers are fine things. Speaking of living, Mary is frying chicken and we're having huckleberry pie."

"Now, that's heaven," Floyd replied.

As they began to walk up the hill, the doctor put his arm around Floyd for the first time. "You know, Floyd, I'm not a church-goer, but if there is an Almighty that made these mountains, then there has to be a reason for us to be here, and that reason in this hurting world has to be to help people. Be a helper, Floyd. If I've done anything for you, don't be a hurter, be a helper."

After they had returned to the car, Floyd turned and said, "You know, you're a poet, Doc."

The doctor snorted, "Well, if you believed that bull, then you're even dumber than I thought. I just wanted you to get up and get back to work."

A few days later, Floyd was riding Old Cap along the range to check for broken fence lines. There was a peaceful quietness in the shadowy forest, with the soft tread of the horse's hooves being the only sound. It was a drowsy mid-morning ride. Suddenly out of the stillness there came a piercing, angry scream.

Spurring his horse, Floyd dashed out into the open just in time to see a large eagle diving into the sparse underbrush. He rose swiftly and lighted on a high crag, pausing a few moments before starting down toward his prey. A big timber rattler was his target, as it coiled ready to strike its' assailant. The eagle gave another blood-curdling cry as he neared the ground, and with claws spread he landed on the coiled reptile. How help-less the earth-bound snake appeared as it was carried up and up into the sky. Floyd noted a pause in the speed of the great bird, and the mighty wings began to droop, and the two assailants plummeted down toward the ground. Floyd waited for some time before leaving his spooked horse to examine the still bodies of the King of the Sky and the King of the Ground. They were both mangled, as they had struck a granite boulder, and they no longer resembled the arrogance of their former selves. Evidently, the duel had been going on for some time, and during the fight the rattler had bitten the eagle several times. The venom had done its work, and in mid-air the huge bird was rendered helpless, but the great claws had pierced and torn the writhing snake's body again.

The rattlers were added to Floyd's collection, and some large eagle feathers were also taken to show the men in the bunkhouse, to further verify his story. As he rode along, Floyd began to think of this tragedy and how so many people were like the dueling monarchs. Why can't people come together in this world and help each other, instead of continually trying to dominate and destroy each other?

Talking to the doctor later about this story inspired the doctor to give Floyd his Bible. "I've felt for a long time that this Jesus Christ is the answer. When you read about him, you'll see that's the way God ought to be. I guess I need to observe a good Christian for a while to really believe it. Christianity as Christ lived it would be the most beautiful, inspirational force in the world. Christianity as I've seen it lived is the greatest farce ever perpetrated on unsuspecting mankind. Some of the greatest inhumanity in history has been committed in the name of religion. I've heard the Quakers and the Catholic nuns and the Methodist circuit-riding pastors are real Christians in every way. But I've got to observe one, to see if it's the real thing. Floyd, if I had a son, I would want him to be a real Christian. Would you read the Good Book, and tell me what you find?"

A prayer by Rev. Floyd E. White at age 65:

Oh, Creator of mankind, so teach us to number our days that we may apply our hearts toward Wisdom...and let the beauty of the Lord our God be upon us: and establish thou the work of our hand upon us ...." Help us, Oh God, to learn from the experiences of life so that we may live each day a little better than the day before. In Jesus name we pray.

Amen and Amen.

The Friend That Sticketh Closer Than a Brother

A look at the day
that is slowly being forgotten

A 10-year-old (in 1870) whose father may have served in the Civil War would have lived to see war with Spain in the 1890s and, as a senior citizen, "The war to end all wars" — World War I.

The years between 1870 and 1930 were years of rapid change in the internal life of the country. Not only telephones, but the 5-dollar-a-day wage, and the radio were new. So were the ideas, the values and much of the morality that shaped American life.

Evangelical theology, as well as American society, also underwent a tumultuous 60 years from 1870–1930. If this period marked the Great Divide in American life, it marked no less a divide for the theology of American Protestants.

The Gospel in America by John D. Woodbridge,
Mark A. Noll and Nathan O. Hatch,
Zondervan Publishing, Grand Rapids, Michigan,
1979, pages 48, 49

The Friend That Sticketh Closer Than a Brother

"In resolution, he plunged himself so deeply in his reading of these books, and through his little sleep and much reading he dried up his brains, and he fell into one of the strangest conceits that ever a madman stumbled on in this world...that he himself should become a knight-errant, and go throughout the world, to seek adventures, and practice in person all that he had read!"

CERVANTES, *The Ingenious Gentleman Don Quixote De La Mancha*

"Humility, meekness, mercy, purity of heart, peacemaking, these are the ideas of a crazy man," Floyd said to his horse. Old Cap moved along quickly, swishing his tail at horse flies and mosquitoes. His iron shoes rang against protruding stones. The path went through the long forest that bordered the river. "Love your neighbor as yourself, love your enemies, joy, peace, patience, kindness, goodness, faithfulness, gentleness, self control — it's ridiculous, Cap, only a fool would try to live like that." Floyd took off his hat, wiping the sweat off his forehead with the sleeve of his shirt. "Can you imagine how a person would be used and abused if they tried to live like that? They would be trampled! Although I have to admit, I like the style of this man, Jesus. He certainly lived what he believed. Maybe a person who has been a church-goer their whole life might lean this way, but a messed-up nobody like me could never dream of following this Jesus. Isn't that right, Cap?" Cap snorted and continued swatting flies as if to say, "I'm just a cow pony, don't ask me."

Floyd and the doctor spent many a late night by the fire talking about the feasibility of these words of Jesus. Both of them agreed that they were wonderful ideas, but a painfully impossible way to live in the modern world of 1916. Why, cars were practically in every town, electricity was all over the place, and there was even a telephone where they could talk over wires. And to top it all off, man could even fly! The doctor was 60 years old, and there had been all those changes in his lifetime. The world had grown up since his Civil War childhood. It appeared as though mankind had outgrown the ability to live by these naive Christian ideals.

The more Floyd thought about the meaning of life, the more miserable he became. Why did some kids get to grow up in wealthy, perfect homes and others barely got by?

Privately, Floyd and Edna were not on speaking terms. Floyd honestly felt like he hated Edna. Somebody had to hate her; she certainly deserved it. Floyd had come a long way since those hard times when he was 10 years old. He loved the Collisters as well as his real mom and family. Through the events of his life, he had come to the conclusion that he had been the sole cause of his loneliness and despair. He felt in many ways as though he continued to live in the dark shadow of loneliness, as much now as ever. Finally, Floyd discarded the doctor's Bible, believing that this was the only way he would find peace of mind.

One late November evening as the light was fading, Floyd took careful aim with his gun. His insides felt cold. Both loneliness and sadness gripped him, and he felt as if they would sap his soul of any goodness. When he had Old Cap's temple in the sights of the gun, and his finger on the trigger, his horse nickered at him one last time. Floyd lowered the gun and began to sob, tightly hugging the gray-white horse that lay at his feet.

The terrible accident replayed in Floyd's mind. Now it seemed beyond reason to hope that anything could prevent the horse from falling into the deep canyon. The trail had been extremely icy, and the horse had slipped several times. He had watched as his friend slid over the edge of the trail to the ledge where he was now lodged under a fallen tree. Cap had slid about 300 feet below the trail, where he now lay, quivering helplessly. There was a sick feeling in the pit of Floyd's stomach, as he could not even pretend to hope that he could rescue his friend.

"Please, God, he's been my guardian angel, we can't give up on him." Floyd thought how strange it felt to pray when he wasn't sure if he even believed. But stranger yet was the feeling that God was listening, and that He really cared.

Floyd scrambled up the steep incline and started down the trail, slipping and sliding, sometimes searching for the path on his hands and knees in black, mountain darkness. At last, he saw a faint light and found a ranch house. When he knocked on the door, and talked to them, the rancher and his two sons could see how important this young man's horse was to him. They supplied ropes, axes, a saw, and two good lanterns. As they approached the horse, there was again that nicker as it seemed to say, "Thank you for coming back."

Working by the light of the lanterns, they sawed the log to roll it off the horse. Determining that Cap's legs were not broken, they urged him to stand, and he responded at once. To get him off the ledge, he had to be turned around on his hind feet, with his front feet over the chasm. They dug a place on the hillside for him to lie down and rest until morning. On long trips, Floyd always carried some oats in his saddlebag, and he gave Cap some before they returned to the ranch to wait for morning. Removing the saddle and placing it beside the trail, they started back to the rancher's home to spend the night.

The next morning, Floyd went back to get his horse, but he was gone. Floyd never forgot how heavy the saddle and blankets were as he carried them back to the ranch. When he finally approached the ranch, Old Cap greeted him with that familiar nicker as he approached the corral. Nobody will ever know how Old Cap ever scrambled up the steep mountainside.

As if the Lord had answered his prayer, Floyd found himself going back to the "Good Book" to continue his search. The ninety-first Psalm seemed to put into words his feelings that dark night when he had almost lost Old Cap.

> *He that dwelleth in the secret place of the most High shall abide under the shadow of the Almighty. There shall no evil befall thee...for he shall give his angels charge over thee, to keep thee in all thy ways.*

Floyd felt his body fill with the burning fire of faith as he said out loud, "This is mine!" His eyes sparkled with tears, and his brain filled with wonder that he should be so aware of God's existence and His love. He read the last part of that old passage where now it speaks from God to the reader.

He shall call upon me, and I will answer him: I will be with him in trouble; I will deliver him and honor him. With long life will I satisfy him, and show him my salvation.

Floyd's search continued until he found himself on a cold bright moonlit winter night riding Old Cap through deep snow. Old Cap's strength and maturity were essential as he reared up, breaking the crust of the snow. He continued to fight valiantly to break the trail, and Floyd knew that in this frigid weather his life depended on his horse's courage.

Was it luck that wise Old Cap had been chosen for the cross-country ride to hear the Methodist circuit pastor? Floyd was now the foreman of the ranch, and he had several horses to choose from. He now rarely rode Old Cap, except for pleasure. His fastest horse was a young filly, which was usually chosen for the 20-mile ride into Sweet. Yet for some reason, tonight he could not catch the wily animal. He chose instead his trustworthy mount, Old Cap. Now Floyd was thankful as the young mare could never have broken through the crust of the snow.

The ranch hands all admired Floyd and had shared many adventures with him. They had been willing to finish the cattle feeding in order for him to get an early start to town. Floyd didn't tell them he was going to a church meeting, for they would have had a good laugh if they knew.

The Idaho countryside was beautiful in the winter. The towering mountains pointed to heaven. The frosted trees and the glittering icicles testified to the sacredness and cathedral-likeness of creation. The soft singing from the plain white chapel interrupted the stillness of the mountainside.

The snow in the mountain village of Sweet, Idaho, looked like a Christmas card as Floyd rode into town. Floyd put his tired horse in the warm livery stable, and asked the liveryman to give him a rubdown and a good feed. Then he walked toward the tavern for supper. He would let the meeting get rolling before he attended. He was cold and hungry, and the waitress was slow. Floyd thought, "I hope that Methodist pastor has a long sermon, or I'll never make it."

A power capsule inspired by Ephesians 3:16

I pray that out of his glorious riches he may strengthen you with power through his Spirit in your inner being.

To change on the outside, let God work on the inside!

(God starts with the deeper issues, not just the symptoms!)

Floyd had heard that this tall pastor was a real man as well as a real Christian, and he knew it was time to investigate first-hand this Christian way.

Floyd admired the ideals of love, peace, and hope that were in the Christian message. He felt that an idealist truly committed to this way would face a great challenge, but a life of following this Jesus would have to help many people. It all seemed impossible to Floyd, but he sensed God's existence, and desperately felt a need for His companionship.

When he had finished his meal, he walked to the chapel. The preacher was in full swing with his sermon, and not only was every seat taken, but people were also standing, and others were leaning against the walls. This was where Floyd now stood, taking off his hat. Several young cowboys from the area were there. The revival meetings had been going on for two weeks, and this was the climactic last night. The preacher talked about Jacob and the loneliness he felt as he lost every-thing, and when he left home in search of the meaning of his life. The preacher told how Jacob was all alone, and how he wrestled with God. Floyd felt his jaw began to tremble as the words cut right to his heart, and he hoped nobody noticed. In his altar call for those who were making the decision to follow Christ, the preacher singled out one man. "If you would only surrender to the call of God, how many lives would be influ-enced? God created you for a reason, you are not a mistake." The preacher's eyes flashed as he spoke. "How many lonely, hurting people could you help, if you walked with Jesus Christ...*the friend that sticketh closer than a brother?*"

The pastor boldly asked for the impossible. "Commit all your heart right now to live in the light of love, instead of darkness and bitterness toward life. Spend the rest of your days encour-aging people and serving them, instead of judging them, and living in despair. Dare to be a Christian. Walk up here in front of the whole town and kneel at this altar, admit your sins and mistakes — turn to God."

Floyd thought how embarrassing it would be if he became a Christian and everyone found out. He thought that he would have to give up all his girlfriends, and probably would have trouble finding a pretty Christian girl to date. He thought of the people who would take advantage of a sincere believer. He glanced over at what he thought was the meanest, dirtiest cow-boy in town. "God, if You can reach him, there is no question that You're there. I don't know what I am saying! I'm praying again."

The crowd began to sing.

> *Just as I am without one plea,*
> *But that thy blood was shed for me,*
> *And that thou biddest come to me,*
> *O lamb of God, I come. I come.*

The tough cowboy Floyd was looking at began to cry as he got up to walk in front of this little country church. The crowd sang on.

> *Just as I am, and waiting not,*
> *To rid my soul of one dark blot,*
> *To thee whose blood can cleanse each spot,*
> *O lamb of God, I come, I come.*

Floyd began to walk toward the front, his spurs clinking with each step. The congregation was visibly shocked to see the two rough, wayward cowboys responding. It would have been more likely to see them fighting across the street in the tavern than walking toward the altar. The emotion in the voices could be heard as the church kept on singing even louder and more joyously.

> *Just as I am, though tossed about,*
> *With many a conflict, many a doubt,*
> *Fighting fears within, without,*
> *O lamb of God, I come! I come!*

As Floyd walked toward the front he saw some cowboys laughing, but he didn't care. He saw some church ladies gossiping, but he didn't care. He saw some children staring, wide-eyed, as they were impressed by the power of God to reach a cowboy like Floyd. He knelt at the altar. The sense of tragedy for his life that he had always felt left that night. He prayed, "Oh Jesus, if you could come into my life and make some sense and reason out of a life like mine." He paused as he choked on his tears. "*I would spend the rest of my life just being amazed at the wonder of it all!*"

His mind flashed back to that lonely coldness that he had felt at 10 years of age, when he looked in the window and saw the reflection of a child. He had become entwined in self-pity, feeling that no one cared. The love of God felt so warm now. He prayed, "Nobody is going to feel that lonely around me! Jesus, you cared for me, and I'm always going to care." Floyd knew then that there was more for him; he was called to be a pastor. For better or for worse, he would spend his life as an idealistic Christian.

The first time he saw Doc Collister after that night, the old Irishman could tell that there was something different about Floyd. The doctor pointed out immediately, "It's happened Floyd, hasn't it?"

Floyd started talking with his head down, and then brought his eyes up shining. "Yes, Doc. I'm a Christian. I went to the Methodist meeting in Sweet, and when the preacher told me about Jesus, I knew deep in my heart that he was God. He told me that Jesus loved me and how he died for me. And I felt so sorry for everything I had done against God. I felt that somehow, just maybe, this love could turn a mistaken life like mine into some beautiful purpose. Then he told me that Jesus was alive, and I knew I had to meet him. I met him at that altar at Sweet Methodist Church. I met Jesus Christ, and I'm going to follow him the rest of my life."

The doctor's old face shone as though it were young again as he looked Floyd right in the eyes and said, "Then we both are, Floyd!" It was some time later that Floyd stuck his head in the ranch house, and asked to speak to the Collisters. He was in his twenties now, and as the foreman of the Collister ranch, he held his head with the confidence that came from the responsibility of leading brave men every day. But he was pale now, because he knew that this would be a difficult moment in his life. Mary Collister looked old and sickly as she came to the door, but her eyes twinkled with the fondness she held for Floyd.

"What is it, Floyd?" she asked, as she could tell that it was serious.

"I just need to talk to you and Doc for a minute," he said, as he fidgeted with his hat. Minutes later, they were all on the porch, and Floyd was trying to speak but he just couldn't.

The doctor interrupted mercifully. "You're going to fight in the Great War, aren't you, Floyd?" Mrs. Collister began to cry.

"Yes, I've got to go. I love this country, I s'pose every one of us does, especially riding around this valley and seeing those mountains. I've got to go…I've just got to go." He looked down as he mumbled his words. "You know I can't thank…"

"You don't have to say anything, we love you, just like you were our own," Mrs. Collister interrupted. She gave Floyd a hug and a soft goodbye as she went back inside, crying.

A meadowlark whistled as the old doctor and the young cowboy stood on the porch. They stood there for what seemed like forever, and yet it didn't seem long enough. The doctor cleared his throat, his lips quivered as he said his last words. "If we don't see you again on earth, we'll see you in glory." The doctor spoke with tears running down his cheeks. They were the first tears Floyd had ever seen from this father figure. Neither one of the men could say much else without completely breaking down, so they clung to their manhood as they shook hands in a false display of formality. The doctor turned and opened the screen door, as Floyd held onto the rail as he descended the steps. Floyd's heart pounded nervously as so many pictures flashed through his mind. He thought of the first time that he had met the doctor, and how intimidated he had been and yet how grateful. His mind replayed the late night runs and the many experiences demonstrating the doctor's commitment to helping people. The hanging and the wise doctor's talk after Floyd had passed out seemed as if it were just yesterday. Timidly, Floyd turned around, and called out, "Doc!" They both walked back together and clumsily hugged for the first and last time. "Thanks," said the cowboy.

"Thank you," said the tough old Irish doctor.

As Floyd walked away from the ranch house, he heard a familiar nicker. Old Cap called to him from the coral, and Floyd slipped him some sugar. "Goodbye, old boy," he said as he patted his head. A still, small voice spoke to the heart of this young Christian. "This is the last time you will see them again on this earth, but you'll never be alone again. I'll be with you always." Floyd lifted his eyes to the familiar mountain peaks as he prayed, "Thank you, Jesus."

A prayer by Rev. Floyd White after
an article telling the story of his new birth:

Our Father, we thank you for Your messengers who have shared with us the Good News of your salvation. And thank you with full hearts that Jesus has been and will always continue to be the friend that sticketh closer than a brother. Quicken us to a deep responsibility to tell others of our Christ. Lift us, Lord, into Your living light, and fill our souls with your presence. In the name of Your Glorious Son.

Amen and Amen.

CHAPTER SIX

The Miracle of Love

Two million dead, a generation lost: world counts cost of its first total war!

DECEMBER 31, 1918

"Blow out, you bugles, over the rich dead!" wrote Rupert Brooke, and Laurence Binyon echoed, in consolation: "They shall not grow old, as we that are left grow old." But that was said before the enormity of the casualties could be guessed at — over 10 million dead, in war cemeteries lining the battlefields like serried battalions of crosses or in unmarked graves at the bottom of the sea.

The cost was a lost generation, and none were more aware of it than the writers on both sides. What passing bells for these who die as cattle?" asked Wilfred Owen. Those who died, either in action or in active service, included Brooke, who came to stand for his generation cut off in the bud of promise, Edward Thomas, Isaac Rosenberg, and Owen, killed a week before the armistice on the western front. His poems, written in the trenches, begin with the words: "My subject is war and the pity of war. The poetry is in the pity."

Some of the survivors, like Siegfried Sassoon, have already made public the uncomfortable view that the lost generation had been sacrificed by incompetent commanders, careless of the lives of those who had to do the dying. Sassoon threw his Military Cross into the River Mersey in protest at the slaughter. His reward was to be dispatched to a mental hospital, diagnosed as shell-shocked.

Chronicle of the World, Jerome Burne, Editor, Chronicle Communications, London, England, page 1071

The Miracle of Love

"Did my lady think to put me to a test?
Ah, sweet sovereign of my captive heart,
I shall not fail thee, for I know.
I have dreamed thee too long,
Never seen thee or touched thee, but known thee
with all of my heart.
If I reach out to thee, Do not tremble and shrink
from the touch of my hand on thy hair.
Let my fingers but see, Thou art warm and alive,
and no phantom to fade in the air.
I have sought thee, sung thee, dreamed thee,
Now I've found thee and the world shall know thy glory!"

Don Quixote to Dulcinea
Dale Wasserman, MAN OF LA MANCHA

It is difficult to fully describe how empty Floyd felt as he returned from the "war to end all wars." The next significant event in his life was when he returned to Boise to meet Edna, after the Collisters had gone on to heaven.

Edna was living in the ranch house with her new husband, who was supposedly a war hero. Floyd had been informed that one-half of the Collister fortune had been left to him, but Edna and her attorneys had the will ruled temporarily invalid. They said that the Collisters were not in their right minds when they left so much to this ranch hand who had left them.

Floyd asked to see Edna in person, and they arranged to meet in Boise at the office of Edna's successful attorney. When Floyd walked into the office, he looked far more confident and experienced than Edna had remembered him. He was still a cowboy, as his Stetson hat and boots testified. Floyd was smiling, as if he had good news to share. The emotions between Edna and Floyd are impossible for us to understand today. They had wavered between a romantic relationship and a mutual hatred when they were growing up. But after Floyd committed his life to Jesus Christ, the direction of their relationship was set in Edna's mind, and it was sheer hatred. She had continued living the wild life that Floyd had been a part of in the past. The years of hard living now showed on her, as evidenced by lips that were bright red, eye shadow so heavy that she looked as if she were painted for war, and her clothes were ostentatious.

Floyd began the conversation saying, "It's good to see you, Edna." Edna didn't answer. Her husband stepped between Floyd and Edna, as if he were prepared to fight. Everything about this man trumpeted a challenge to Floyd, as if two bull Elks were preparing to butt heads.

Edna's husband finally spoke, as he smiled from behind his Teddy Roosevelt mustache. "Listen here, Ephraim," and he paused to see if that would cause the cowboy to lose control. "There is not a thing you can do. We've contested the will and Edna is the only living Collister." Floyd thought about how pleasurable it would be to pop this war hero, and show him how tough a cowboy could be when he got his dander up. But he had chosen his course years ago in Sweet, and now this was an opportunity to test those lofty ideals. As an army veteran, Floyd wasn't easily intimidated. He told the lawyer, "You know that this won't hold up legally. Doc told plenty of people what his plans were."

The high-powered lawyer replied, "Can you afford the challenge?"

Floyd had never backed down from anyone in his life, and he calmly answered. "All I have to do is show my case to another greedy two-bit lawyer, and he'll fund the litigation until I get what we both know I deserve."

The lawyer sat down as if Floyd had popped him one, as did Edna's husband. He looked at her as though he had made a mistake. Edna looked as if she was at a loss, but only for a second. She looked out the window as she began to speak. "I told you years ago, Ephraim, that you would never get an inheritance, and I meant it!" Floyd looked a little taken aback, as he sensed a level of evil and hatred that he had rarely experienced before. She went on, and the tone of her voice reflected the power of her personal wickedness. Unless you have ever stood face-to-face with a truly wicked person, you will never know what Floyd felt as he stood before Edna. She had been his adopted sister, girlfriend, competitor, and devious enemy.

She spoke with almost a growl in her voice. "The most important thing in the world to you is to become a pastor, isn't it... isn't it?" All three men looked a little stunned at this display of villainy. She turned now and attacked Floyd with cold, murderous eyes as she said, "I know every drunken stupor you ever wallowed in, every sinful relationship you ever enjoyed, and every lie you ever told!" Floyd's look told her that all that garbage didn't matter, now that he was a Christian, so she went on. "What church will want a bastard for a pastor? Do you think the Methodists, Presbyterians, or Baptists would be interested in a pastor after I get through telling them about a young cowboy's dark side?"

It would have hurt less if Floyd and the men had fought it out with their fists. Floyd staggered back, visibly showing fear, but Edna kept attacking. Floyd thought, "I could tell her secret — that she is not a Collister." Then the twinges of panic began, because he knew it wouldn't make any difference, she knew how desperate he was to be a pastor. Confusion, panic, hatred, and fear gripped him like a vice. He remembered noticing that the other two men in the room looked upon him with confusion, as this once proud man was now reduced to a groveling supplicant.

Floyd had the idea that maybe people would be big enough to forgive him, but that idea only lasted for a moment.

Years later, he told his grandson that times and attitudes had changed a great deal in a century. His mother had not been a bad person; she had just lived with a man in hard times. People don't think that much about that kind of thing today. The man had left her pregnant in Arkansas, and she later met and married a very good man named Edward White. He had treated Floyd like a son and an accepted member of the White family. His mother lived to be almost 100 years old, and she was always an important person in his life, as were his sisters and brother. All of his problems were

because of his incredible temper. At that time, a birth out of wed-
lock was almost an unforgivable sin, unlike today. The attitude
toward the "illegitimately born" was a kind of morality, controlled
by making them pay social dues throughout their lifetime. Now
whether that was the way it was or not, is not as important as the
fact that this was the way Floyd interpreted the times.

He felt overwhelmed with confusion. This was such a dark
moment, and he felt the prayers he was trying to say under his
breath seemed like they were hitting a brick wall, as if God was
a million miles away. The inheritance would mean financial
security for the rest of his life, and after his impoverished childhood, this was very important to him. He loved life on a ranch,
and he tried out the idea of just being a dedicated layman in
the church. Then he remembered his covenant at Sweet...it
seemed like a world war and a lifetime ago.

His choice was ministry or wealth. Floyd took a deep breath,
as though he were getting ready to dive off a cliff into one of
his favorite ice-cold mountain streams. When he took that
breath, he raised himself again to his full height, and the
courage and idealism returned to his eyes. "Edna, I can't
believe that you could live your whole life with the Collisters
and miss the point."

Edna was taken aback, but she had not lost her source of
power. "No, you don't understand, Ephraim. You get the
point, I get everything else."

Floyd paused and looked around the room as if he was savor-
ing this moment, and he would never forget it as long as he
lived. He smiled and felt free, "Okay, I'll take it. But Edna,
remember — it's never too late to learn to care for people!"

Floyd left the room, closing the door behind him. He walked
out onto the streets of Boise. He thought, "I'm as poor as when

I walked these streets as a boy." Then he said out loud, "No I'm not, I've got my inheritance."

Floyd made his way to the First Methodist Church of Boise, which was later to be called the Cathedral of the Rockies. After speaking to the pastor, Floyd accepted the responsibilities of teaching the youth Sunday school class. Finding a paying job was easy with all of his experience.

A power capsule inspired by Jeremiah 6:16

Stand at the crossroads and look; ask for the ancient paths, ask where the good way is, and walk in it, and you will find rest for your souls.

It's time to relax, enjoy, and let God take over!

(Rest in the Lord and wait patiently for Him; Do not fret.)

Anyone who saw this big cowboy in his twenties could detect his loneliness. Where does an "old" army veteran find Christian girls to date? Floyd tried to forget the subject, but he kept finding himself thinking of the qualities of his illusory future wife. The more he thought of her, the more preposterous the idea became. He wanted someone to share all his life, including his ministry. He envisioned someone who would be beautiful both in spirit and body, someone who would be a fortress of strength of personality for him. He had to have someone with sincerity and a tender love for Jesus. He felt attracted to girls with sophistication and dignity, but also strong women who spoke their mind. He also wanted her to have pretty eyes...the kind a man could get lost in, when he needed to.

As an older single, Floyd felt like he continually stuck out like a sore thumb. Thanksgiving was difficult, and Christmas was positively miserable.

During this time of loneliness, Floyd experienced some consolation in working with young people. There were kids who had lost their fathers in WWI, and Floyd expressed his care by spending hours playing baseball and volleyball with them. He helped them with their homework. He could sense when certain kids had come to believe that they were unintelligent or unattractive. He listened to their doubts, patched their hurts with their parents, and proclaimed the Good News to them on Sundays. Floyd began to work with the youth of several Methodist churches. He had been the Student Body President of Boise High School, and so the kids looked up to him. His reputation as a dynamic young Christian leader spread throughout that part of Idaho. He supported himself in an oil business that was quickly growing in Idaho, while continuing to work with the kids in his ministry. While he could not envision leaving "his" kids, he was missing out on the necessary education to become a full-time minister in the Methodist church.

But his loneliness was dictating his decisions at this point. Nights were the worst for him, and exhaustion wasn't enough to put a lonely young man to sleep. Floyd tossed and turned and tossed some more. One night, it seemed impossible to sleep, so he took a walk under the stars. The night sky was glittering with multitudes upon multitudes of solar systems. As Floyd walked away from the lights of Boise, the smallness of the earth made him feel closer to heaven. The closeness between him and the Almighty was that of two friends who didn't need to speak. Floyd was far enough out of town that he could not be heard, so he sang out loud. He couldn't carry a tune but it felt good to sing.

"My God and I walk through the field together...hand in hand as good friends do."

Floyd knelt in the dirt and prayed.

"Gracious Master, you're so good to me. Thank you for your love... I really need it. But God, I see people with their families and I still feel alone. I hate that feeling...but it has drawn me closer and closer to you, Lord. If it's not out of place, I would like to ask something of you. If you say no, I'll understand."

Emotion swelled like a rising tide within him, and as tears pressed at Floyd's eyes, his throat struggled to stay clear so that he could talk. After the wave had passed, Floyd finally felt like he could say the words from his heart.

"The greatest blessing in the world to me would be a family. A family to love and a ministry with people to care for. That's all I want out of life, God. I don't want or expect anything else in life. And I promise you — I will be content and faithful with this small request. But you know that already. Just help me to see your will more clearly. I love you, Jesus."

Summer camp for the Methodist youth was held at Smith's Ferry on the Payette River. The emerald green water of the Payette sparkled in the white rapids and set off the forest green of the pine trees covering the steep ridges. In those days, everyone would bring their tents and cook their food at camp. Floyd was up on a hill helping some boys in his group put up their tents when the district superintendent came up to talk to him. Although he spoke gruffly, he had a special fondness for Floyd. "White, there are three girls that can't get their tent up. Would you do me a favor and go help them?"

Floyd was a little annoyed at the request as he replied, "Reverend, I've got lots to do here. Couldn't I send some of my kids to help?"

The denominational leader responded to that request with authority. "The Lord has appointed me as your leader, Floyd, and I sense that you ought to set up this tent. Besides, one of the girls is a real flower."

Floyd smiled and said, "I sense that the Lord may be leading you…I'll go!"

As Floyd walked down the hill, he spotted the exact flower that the Superintendent had referred to, and wow, was she beautiful! Her brown hair was full as it shone in the afternoon sun. Her face was pretty as…well, Floyd couldn't put it into words. She had such an aura about her that Floyd remembered thinking that she could have been a Rockefeller, for all he knew. Floyd felt as though this classy young lady was a rare one. His heart began to pound like a teenager on his first date. The closer Floyd got to her, the prettier she looked, and the more nervous he became. This may be hard to understand, but he was more nervous now than he had ever been or ever would be again in his life. That is how much she meant to him, even before he ever spoke to her. Her stunning skin and high cheekbones made Floyd feel like he was outclassed and that he should not get his hopes too high. Finally, he noticed she was just a teenager, and his heart sank, as he was in his late twenties. He said, "Do you girls need some help?" She turned and looked right into his eyes. It was just a moment, but it felt like an hour. He could get lost in her eyes, and in fact, maybe he had. Her laughing brown eyes glittered with life as he searched them.

He was searching those eyes again as we sat next to Grandma's bed as he described the moment that he had fallen in love. The main thing that I noticed now as the two of them relived the scene was that Grandma's eyes were glittering now because of the tears. I thought, "Everyone deserves to be described that way at least once in the presence of the one they love." Grandpa continued to remember and we all leapt back across the century.

Her voice sounded like it came from his dreams or his prayers. Floyd thought, "This is ridiculous, I've fallen head over heels in love with this teenage girl." Floyd searched for a reply to her objection as to his help with the tent. "The District Superintendent of the Methodist Church of Idaho instructed me to help you, I don't think that we should cross him...he does represent the Lord, you know." They all laughed. Floyd thought about how good it made him feel to hear her laugh.

After setting up the tent, Floyd talked her into sneaking away to a restaurant to eat, so they could skip the camp food. She agreed, and brought along two friends.

For the duration of the camp, Floyd was embarrassed by his feelings for her, and he didn't even know her name. Everyone could see the way he felt. He thought, "I've wanted to fall in love since I was a teenager, and now that I've fallen in love I wish I hadn't." Everyone teased Floyd, and he denied it. He hoped that Ione couldn't tell and yet he hoped that she could. When he found out that she was only 17, he decided to forget her. But he kept staring, as if his eyes were not listening to the commands of his brain.

For the remainder of time at the camp, he simply admired Ione from afar as he struggled within and tried to give up his feelings for her. He felt so strongly for her that he was afraid of being hurt. No, a better description would be devastation. It didn't take much intelligence to figure out that Ione did not feel the same way about him. Ione was interested, but she did not feel as though she loved him in the least bit. In fact, she knew that her Dad would not approve of him.

As the camp ended, Floyd reasoned that he would just get to know her a little. As a friend, of course. He searched around the camp to find her, but she had left early to catch a train home.

As Ione sat by the window of the train looking at the rugged Idaho wilderness, she thought of how Floyd wasn't like anyone that she had ever met before. There was something very different about that man. Suddenly, a lady in the train screamed and the people stood up and they were looking out the opposite side of the train. Ione stood up and looked out the other side, to see a car wildly driving alongside the train. The crazy man driving the car was waving a flag as he dodged trees and cattle. When Ione saw who the wild man was, she sat back down and blushed. It was Floyd. The car drove up by the engine and flagged down the train. The engineer stopped the train, cussing up a storm as he yelled, "This had better be an emergency!"

Floyd yelled back angrily, "It is an emergency!"

Ione just sat there blushing, and the people were murmuring as Floyd stepped onto the train. He came up to Ione and grabbed her by the shoulders, gently standing her up. Everyone was staring, and most of the women were smiling. Floyd took off his hat, saying, "What's your name and where do you live?"

She smiled, and then she laughed as the train started going again. She chuckled out the words, "It looks like you're going with me, anyway." Floyd turned to get ready to jump off. She yelled out, "Ione Fee, Fruitland, Idaho! My dad's name is James Fee." Floyd smiled and jumped. Ione sat back down.

The lady in front of her commented, loud enough so that everyone could hear, "That certainly was an unusual man." Ione smiled as she said to herself. "He certainly is!"

Grandma sat up in her bed and took Grandpa's hand and said, "Oh, Floyd, I've had my moments when I was sorry that you have your crazy side, but I'm glad that you chased down that train!" I said, "I am too, Grandpa." Grandma began to take the story from there, and for a while there were no arguments as to the details.

Ione hadn't been home very long when a box of candy arrived with a note and only a few words.

> *Ione,*
> *I love you!*
> *Floyd Edward White*

After many more letters and a whole bunch of dates, Floyd was called to preach at the Sunday evening service of Fruitland Methodist Church, and Ione attended. Afterward, they went for a walk at the Weiser Park. As they walked under the stars, Floyd felt like they were the same stars that had been overhead when he had requested that the Lord send him someone just like Ione. He told Ione about his life, his deepest hurts, and his secret. He talked about love and hope. He talked about humility, gentleness, meekness, purity, servitude, and making peace in the world. Ione looked so beautiful under the stars, and her eyes twinkled as she told Floyd that she loved him. They kissed and sat on a bench. Floyd got down on his knees as he asked, "Ione, will you marry me?" A tear ran down her cheek as she answered him. "No, Floyd." Floyd was crushed. He wasn't the type of man to get on his knees unless he was praying, and he just looked humiliated down there as he was looking for a graceful way to get up. How do you take a rejection like that while you're on your knees? Neither Floyd nor Ione could speak…they didn't know what to say. Floyd took Ione home without either of them so much as muttering a word, and he returned to Boise emotionally crushed and confused.

Floyd was numb for a couple of days until he received a letter from Ione. This letter only had one important word, and was written in the same style that Floyd had used in his courting notes to Ione.

Floyd,
Yes!
Ione Octavia Fee

Floyd immediately traveled to the Fee home. The Fee family had lived for years in Knoxville, Iowa, but had moved to Idaho when Ione's sister Grace came down with tuberculosis. Her doctor had advised that the weather of Idaho might be better for her. Ione's father had gone to college with George Washington Carver, and now owned a successful farm. The Fees were a Christian family. Ione's father, James Fee, had walked the sawdust trail during an evangelistic meeting held by a former pro-baseball player and reformed alcoholic. That evangelist's name was Billy Sunday, and the course of the Fee family had been changed on that night. Ione had gone to the altar at seven years of age and was baptized a Presbyterian, but the family became Methodist after they moved to Idaho.

When Floyd arrived at the Fee home, Ione's father answered the door. She asked her Dad if she and Floyd could speak to each other alone. Floyd interrupted, "Sir, I've asked your daughter to marry me." James Fee looked at Floyd rather intensely, but Floyd didn't waver a bit. Finally, Mr. Fee showed his teeth behind his mustache and his smile eased the tension of both Floyd and Ione. "Floyd, you're a fine man and a sure Christian. I can't argue with Ione, and I'll be surprised if you'll be able to, either."

They went into the other room and sat together as Ione started to speak, but Floyd stopped her. He looked agonized by what he was going to say. "When I asked you to marry me and you said no, I was so ashamed, so humiliated." Ione's eyes filled with tears as she took his big hand in hers. "Floyd, I'm so young, and it's all been so fast, so intense."

Floyd continued his important words. "It has been fast, so let me explain some things. Ione, I have nothing to offer you but hardship and poverty." Tears were in his voice as he spoke. "I want to be a pastor. That means we'll never have money or nice things, there will be calls in the middle of the night, there will always be someone dying and people will always be criticizing us, people will demand my time, and feel jealous of you." Ione tried to interrupt, "Floyd." But he wouldn't be interrupted, so he continued. "Anytime we buy anything nice, people will make us feel guilty about it, and to top it all off, I want as many kids as possible. But when I'm with you, I feel I can do anything. I want to try and bring peace to the world. I want to make it a better place for our children. I want to wake up to look into your eyes every morning of my life."

"Floyd," Ione interrupted with enough power of personality to finally stop him. "I love you...I know that you want those things. As long as we have each other and the Lord, we'll be all right!"

The early years of their marriage were blessed. Floyd continued to work for the Goodman Oil Company, with the promise of becoming a partner. God blessed them financially, and they continued to minister where they could in the church. During these early days, God blessed them with two boys. They were hoping to save enough money to go to seminary. The oil business was going very well along with everything else, but Floyd was miserable. Finally, one evening he came home after a long day at work, looking as if a mule had kicked him. Ione knew it was serious.

"What's the matter, Hon?" she questioned.

"Things weren't right at work, and I quit," he said in an uncharacteristically weak voice.

Ione sat down, looking completely exasperated. Floyd prepared for a fight. When Ione wanted to argue she knew how to win, both intellectually and emotionally. Allen and Jimmy began to cry, sensing something was wrong. Ione picked up Jimmy and walked out on the porch. Floyd followed, holding Allen. "Floyd, I'm pregnant, and times are hard." They both just stood there in silence. "What are we going to do, Floyd?"

Floyd's voice became excited. "I'm going into the ministry full-time."

Ione questioned, "Floyd, you don't even have your degree, what church will want you?"

Floyd answered, "The District Superintendent says I can go to the New Meadows Church."

Ione pointed out, "That mountain church doesn't have enough people to support a pastor, and that's why they've never had one. Besides, most of those people hate religion, which is why so few of them go to church."

Floyd paused to let Ione settle down, then said, "People hate because they hurt. I know what it's like to hurt and to hate. That's the church that needs me, and I suppose I need them. I've got to do it, Ione, it's my calling."

Ione replied from the strength of her personality, "Well, it's not my calling, and Floyd you haven't answered me. How will we do it?"

Floyd answered what they both knew. "I don't know!"

Grandma explained to me that throughout their ministry she had been an anchor around Grandpa, as she never really liked many things about the ministry. Grandpa explained it another way. She was the anchor that kept him from getting into too much trouble. Together they had navigated quite a life, and they had adventured through some pretty tough storms while delivering some terrific goods.

Grandma started the "cold war" that they often used as a means of communication in times like this. Finally, one day as they stood on the porch she sighed. This always meant that she was surrendering to what she felt was God's leadership, even if she wasn't going to like it. She lifted her eyes to the mountains and quoted her life verse, "I will lift my eyes to the hills from whence cometh my strength, my strength cometh from the Lord who made heaven and earth." She took Floyd's hand in her hand, and her eyes twinkled as they did the first time they met. "In your heart, Floyd White, there has always been enough for both of us. There is enough love for a person who tends to be a bit practical and cold like me. There is enough hope and power to chase away anything that would keep you from God's calling for our family. I don't know how we will make it. You have poured out your heart to me plenty of times since I met you, and you always surprise me, Floyd Edward White. When you preach there may be many people who don't think you're that great, but all I hear is your heart, Floyd, and I love you for it. What I'm saying is, yes. The ministry is the only place in the world for a person with a heart like yours, and I'll do my best to keep up, just for the privilege of sharing that heart of yours."

The following prayer was written for use at the close of a devotional by Ione Octavia White, April 30, 1981:

Gracious and loving Father, we thank you for the love and understanding of friends and family. Give us quick and tender consciousness of the need for friendship of those around us. Grant that we will always be ready to reach out a friendly hand to the lonely, the forgotten, and the stranger within our gates. And thank you, oh Father, for the rare and lovely people, who having known pain and loneliness, and are able to rise above such conditions and soar in spirit to heights of loving joy. Help us to be conscious of your powerful presence throughout all the days of our lives. Grant us a new sensitivity to others' trials because we have learned from some brave person the true meaning of being thankful. Thank you, Lord, for the warm love and friendship we have with you, our Savior.

Amen and Amen.

CHAPTER SEVEN

People Who Hate God and the Pastor Who Loved Them

Mega church!

CHRISTIANITY TODAY, MARCH 5, 1990

*Marketing savvy and jumbo parking lots have
combined to produce a new breed of big churches.*

"Today 1 in every 300 Lutheran parishes qualifies as a mega church, as does 1 in every 200 Southern Baptist churches, 1 in every 600 United Methodist Churches, 1 in every 100 Assemblies of God congregations, 1 in every 250 congregations affiliated with the American Baptist Church in the U.S.A., and 1 in every 300 churches that carry the word Presbyterian in its name. The emergence of the mega church is one of the four or five most significant developments in contemporary American Church."

Lyle Schaller, page 20

"We pray that before long, leaders of today's biggest church will have built up a spirit-filled reservoir of common wisdom that will allow them to solve the mega church's problems and keep its ministry in focus."

David Neff, page 10

*...Perhaps part of that focus is to remember again the
ministry in the church from the last century.*

People Who Hate God and the Pastor Who Loved Them

"Hear me now, oh thou bleak and unbearable world!
A knight with his banners all bravely unfurled
Now hurls down his gauntlet to thee!
For a holy endeavor is now to begin,
And virtue shall triumph at last!
I am I, Don Quixote, The Lord of La Mancha
My destiny calls and I go;
And the wild winds of fortune will carry me onward,
Oh withersoever they blow,
Onward to glory I go!"

Dale Wasserman, MAN OF LA MANCHA

The old Buick sped along the dirt road through the mountain canyon to New Meadows, Idaho. The morning sun was beginning to cast its warming light into the valley. The tall fir trees along the rough roadway hid the view of the shadowy, winding road, adding a feeling of mystery to every turn. Eagerness and suspense were building for the White family as they approached the mountain valley where they would begin their ministry. Every rut in the road and every sharp rock that the tires bumped over added to the feeling of adventure. "Drive carefully, Floyd, the boys are still sleeping," Ione pleaded. Floyd rolled his eyes; he could never drive well enough to avoid Ione's need to help him.

As the car pulled into the valley, Allen, Jimmy, and Johnny all woke up to the splendor of the magic moment. Floyd pulled the car off the road onto the meadow grass. "Boys, look at those deer," Floyd said, as he reached back and grabbed the baby, John. "Look at that big buck." A buck, two does, and a fawn stopped eating the green meadow grass and stared with innocent brown eyes at this unfamiliar family.

Ione got out of the car and took a deep breath as she said with sparkling eyes, "Oh, Floyd, this is the place, this is God's country." The rich, sweet fragrance of fruit tree blossoms filled the clean mountain air with the aroma of life. The green fir trees speckled the valley as various dainty wild flowers growing at their roots colored the scene with majestic delicacy. The walls of the valley seemed as if it were purposefully decorated with the spring fruit tree blossoms.

Allen and Jim ran after the deer, chasing them away as Floyd stepped out of the car. The look on his face testified to the great expectations that filled his mind. He thought of matching his faith against the coming challenges. "Maybe one of these farm boys will grow up and become another Billy

Sunday, and I will have the privilege of introducing him to Jesus," Floyd exclaimed. Imaginary champions were in every farmhouse as Floyd said, "Let's get going, I can't wait to meet these people."

While the little mountain village of New Meadows was beautiful, it was an unlikely place for a church. For the most part, these mountain people had little room for religion. People lived in the mountains for a reason, and that reason was that they were not particularly fond of people in general. They liked each other well enough, but not outsiders.

Several evangelists had visited the church, holding revivals. All kinds of gimmicks were used to get the people into the church in order that their souls could be saved. The down-to-earth farmers tried religion under pressure from their wives, and they were scolded for their sin. They left church convinced that they would burn forever in the fires of Hell.

Most of the people in that valley had spent their lives in New Meadows. They had known hypocrites who had been so spiritual, and yet they had cheated in business and in their marriages. Such events were impossible to hide in a small community, and memories like that lingered for generations. The con artists who traveled the countryside holding revivals and taking offerings from weeping sinners had also visited New Meadows. The mountain farmer's life was a hard one, and lazy, heavenly minded people talking about the destruction of earth and the renouncing of physical pleasure just rubbed these mountain people the wrong way. Those glassy-eyed, unrealistic Christians constantly pronouncing judgment were not welcome in this valley. It was true that these people refused to attend church. Their language could be described as "barnyard proper," and they were particularly fond of persecuting Christians. Hypocrites, injustice in the world, and the inevitable scars from the unfairness of life itself brought a poisonous bitterness to the hearts of these people. Many had lost promising crops to early frosts. Most had been crushed at one time or another by the death of a child at birth. Losing a spouse to mountain fever had devastated some. In such times of crisis, they had cried to God, begging for His help. When the tragedy struck they literally hated this unknown God.

Floyd and Ione soon found that they were the ministers of a near-empty church that could not afford to support a pastor. A few loyal Methodists had built a white country chapel, but that was all there was to New Meadows Methodist church. If life was hard for the farmers, it was even more difficult for the young pastor's family. Floyd and Ione learned to depend on God as they received their pay in farm produce. One Methodist farmer gave them an apple tree from his orchard. Another Methodist farmer gave them a cow that would supply milk for the boys through the years. The White family received hay, eggs, older chickens and vegetables for pay. Rarely did they know where their next week's food would come from, and many times they received food just before mealtime.

Ione remembered these days in beautiful New Meadows as the very best in her life. She and Floyd grew deeper in their love for each other and in their relationship with Jesus Christ. These days were tough for Ione, as she had never gone without in her childhood — James Fee had made sure of that. She often complained to Floyd about how they were treated by the people, and she worked hard throughout her life to make this major adjustment. It was especially hard for Floyd to have to depend on the leftovers of other people for their livelihood. He had fought all of his life for his independence, and now he was forced to lose it.

In this great test, Floyd and Ione were being pushed and watched by the mountain people to see if they were really the idealistic Christians they professed to be. Under this pressure, Floyd never lost touch with the fact that God had called him into the ministry and that the Almighty was his boss, not the people. Nor did Floyd forget that he was there to serve the people. When a farmer got in a pinch, Floyd helped feed their livestock or harvest the crops. When someone was sick, Floyd not only visited them, but he would often cut their firewood. And when Floyd preached, he encouraged the people during those difficult times. Unaware of theological trends, he simply shared the Good News of Christ's life, death and resurrection. He excelled at telling Bible character sketches and he always made them practical, providing insight into daily living. He rarely preached hellfire and damnation. He felt that he would win more of those mountain people with the mighty love of God, so he always treated them with gentleness and respect. He figured that this was the way Jesus would minister. The sinners of the community felt comfortable coming to church, and many of them found a personal faith in Jesus Christ. When a farmer missed church, Floyd never made them feel guilty, for he knew that it might take several years to reach them again. After all, look how long it took for his faith to break ground after the seeds had been planted in his life. The people began to respect Floyd, and the main reason was because he respected them.

One Sunday morning, the New Meadows High School football coach limped into church. "I've broken my leg, Reverend White, and I can't coach this year," he said. "Those boys have worked hard, and they need a man by their side to rally around. Would you be their coach?"

Floyd looked astonished. "I don't know very much about football," he replied.

The coach patted him on the back, "But you do know something about people and about life. You're elected, all the boys want you."

Every high school football game was a town holiday in that part of the country, and the field was immaculately prepared. The crisp fall air was at its best on sunny Saturday afternoons. The whole town turned out to view the thrilling combat in which their young men would take part. A young man's heroics on the football field would be remembered as long as he lived in the valley. The band from the school rose to each occasion, with patriotic marches and soul-stirring school songs. The smell of fresh caramel apples and hot buttered popcorn added to the flavor of each town football festival.

Football in those days was a tough sport: no helmets or pads, no passing, just hitting. The games meant so much to the town, and there was a lot of pressure on the boys. Floyd sensed that pressure, and gave them the confidence that they needed to play their very best, because he loved them. Many of the skills that Floyd had learned while leading men as a foreman of the Soldier Creek Cattle Ranch came in handy. He had taught those cowboys how to bulldog the orneriest bull, and when he demonstrated on a real live bull, they became unafraid of tackling anybody. Those New Meadow High School farm boys began to see themselves as the toughest group of cowboys in Idaho, and they stuck together through some pretty tough games. When the boys made mistakes, Floyd never lost confidence in them. When a teenager makes a bad mistake and someone stands by them, loving them and believing in them, a relationship with incredible loyalty is forged. No one in the valley had ever seen such a positive coach. The force of Floyd's will seemed to move that team over one challenge after another, until they were ready to play for New Meadows' first conference championship. The championship was to be decided in the final game of the season against their archrival.

Both of the towns held weeklong festivities. Farming in that valley practically came to a halt for that week. Pranks between both towns started out as practical jokes, but ended in a few fistfights.

Game day was a cold, rainy day in November, and the weather seemed to darken the mood of the crowd. Prior to going to the field, Floyd gave his kids a sermon from David and Goliath. He held a stick in front of them showing the height of this 9-foot monster. He told them about a boy with faith who defeated this giant in terrible conflict. As the boys left the school, the opposing team seemed small by comparison. But as Floyd and the boys ran to that dark, muddy field surrounded by the mountain people, they had the distinct feeling that they really were going into all-out war. The rough spectators were hurling shouts and insults across the field.

Both teams lined up and the coaches met in the middle of the field. The opposing coach spoke first, "Reverend White, we've got a big problem here. The referees haven't shown up, and if we cancel this game we could have a riot with the final outcome resulting in both of us being tarred and feathered."

Floyd started laughing, "You're given to exaggeration. You should be a preacher."

The other coach said sternly, "You don't understand. I've lived here my entire life, and these people take their games seriously." Floyd looked at the crowd that was still shouting curses and insults. The other coach kept talking, telling about the football riots they had when Teddy Roosevelt was president. Some people were even killed. Floyd knew that there were some who felt that football should be made illegal in this country just because of events like that. Floyd looked at the crowd again and started to agree. These mountain people looked much tougher now than they did in church.

Floyd laughed nervously as he commented, "Well, what do you suggest that we do? We can't play without a referee."

This time the other coach laughed as he said, "That's for 'hot dang' sure. Whoops, excuse me, parson." He continued rather sheepishly, "There's only one thing that we can do, you've got to be the ref. You're the parson. Can you possibly think of anyone more respected?"

"But I'm not impartial," replied the cowboy pastor.

This time the other coach laughed a big belly laugh as he said cynically, "There is no impartiality in this valley."

As a thunderstorm rolled into the valley, the game began with prayer. It still didn't quiet the townspeople down. The New Meadows team was ready to take on Goliath and they took the ball on their opening drive and pushed it down the throats of the other team. Eventually, the New Meadows fullback broke into the end zone for the first touchdown and an opponent lowered his head and drove into the boy, smashing him to the ground. That vicious tackle took place long after the touchdown play, and both teams broke into an all-out fistfight. The coaches finally pulled their teams apart and took a time out. Floyd stood over by the bench in the middle of his boys, with his black preacher's hat dripping a perpetual waterfall from the rain.

"Men...I call you men because you are men. I would like to tell you that the cheap shots will end when you go back out on that field." Floyd's hoarse voice was at full volume and the boys still had trouble hearing him over the rain and the crowd. Floyd looked around, and a couple of the boys had blood running from their noses, covering their mouths and jerseys. Others had black eyes, and one boy had lost a tooth, and his mouth was bleeding. Another boy had already left the field on the opening drive with a broken arm. Floyd handed his handkerchief to a boy who had a broken nose. Then he spoke to all of them. "You know as well as I do that the cheap shots are going to continue. You're in a fight — a battle — and you might as well recognize it as that. And this time boys, I'm not going to be able to stand by you on the sidelines to pick you up when you get knocked on your rear. I'm a pastor first and foremost, and I've been drafted to be the referee, and to try to keep peace in the valley. In fact, this is my last talk of the game, and of the season. It won't look right for the ref to coach." One of the boys smirked as if they were being abandoned. His dad had abandoned that boy two winters ago. Floyd lifted his chin and looked him in the eye as he talked to the whole team. "But this is the pastor's team, and you are all my boys. So I want you to play like Sunday school boys. No cheap shots on our part. But if you're going to play like Christians, then you won't back down from anyone or anything. Look inside of yourselves and above, to find the guts to prove that justice will prevail — that right is mighty powerful — that goodness is stronger than cheap shots."

Floyd paused as the thunder rolled across the mountain sky. The rain hammered on their heads and the ground as it began to turn to hail. The pause must have been a minute and a half, as Floyd looked at the courage in those teenagers' eyes. "Bigger than this game is what takes place in your hearts. It's a tough world out there, and right doesn't always win. Gentleness and goodness are not always strong enough. But for me and my boys, that's the way we'll go down, believing and standing for the best and sticking to it with all of the courage we can muster. Now, make me proud of you. Let's pray.

"Our Father who art in heaven. Hallowed be this game. Thy kingdom come thy will be done on the field as well as in the church. Give us this game — our daily bread, and forgive us our sins as we forgive the opponents. Lead us into the courage to do the right with all of our might. For thine is the kingdom and the power and the glory forever. Most of all — let us play with a heart that will give you glory. Amen and Amen."

The hitting grew more intense as the weather grew worse. The rain and hail were pounding the field so hard that they could hardly see the game, and the clouds robbed the sky of light. Neither team scored through the first half.

Floyd refused to give his team a half-time talk, he just stood alone in the middle of the field, praying. His black preacher's hat and overcoat gave a ghostly silhouette to the coach-less boys as they stared at their pastor from afar.

Floyd prayed, "Either way Lord — this could be my last day in the valley."

The game was brutal. Toward the end of the game, one of the other teams' players picked up a fumble and ran 80 yards for the tying touchdown. Floyd waved his arms. "No touchdown, I'm calling that back," he yelled.

"What?" The opposing coach ran at him cussing like he would kill him. A mountain farmer tackled Floyd, and fists were swinging all over as fights erupted and chaos prevailed. Finally, the other coach, seeing the riot that he had started, yelled for quiet. "Let's hear him out before we continue."

Floyd got up and straightened his coat as he wiped the blood off his lip. "I don't tell lies; I'm a pastor first and foremost. That man was down," he said, with all of the strength and sincerity that he could muster.

One farmer screamed, "Yeah, that call makes your team win."

The opposing coach yelled, "Goll darn it, Floyd, nobody saw him go down." No one on either team or in the crowd could support Floyd's call, even though they all knew that the visibility made it almost impossible to see.

"I saw him go down," said the pastor. "Come on, I'll show you." As Floyd walked, he hoped the mark would be there. On the ground, at the spot of the play, there was a perfect knee mark in the mud. "Now, where is the boy?" asked the pastor. The boy was a substitute with a clean uniform, except for his knee.

The other coach looked right at Floyd, "You've got more guts than any man I've ever met, pastor. I'll be in church Sunday."

That Sunday, New Meadows First Methodist Church was full of people. It reminded Floyd of the revival in Sweet where he met his Savior. Floyd took time early in the service to share his understanding of Christianity.

"The Good News of Jesus Christ is a mighty wonderful thing. It's much more wonderful than Christians have sometimes given it credit for over the years. In fact, it's more wonderful than any of us can fully understand. I guess you can't fully appreciate what I'm saying unless you've really been hurt at some time in your life, and touched by the warmth of God's love.

"John Wesley, the founder of the Methodist Church, said, 'The world is my parish.' Well, this valley is our parish. That means we are supposed to be there for all the people, not just the people in church. If we are going to follow Jesus, then we need to learn to help people. Because I'm sure that is what he would do if he were here. And he is here, inside of us. I'm a Christian because I finally heard the Good News. In fact, I saw the Good News in Christians.

"Whether you are working a cattle ranch or working a farm, we all have learned that it's not what a person says that counts, it's what he does. Any city slicker can talk a day's work, and we all know enough not to pay attention to a person like that. That's because most folks are country folk, no matter what country, they're waiting for a day's work. And what is a day's work? It's being gentle with people who don't believe, just the way a good Methodist would. It's reaching out first to build a friendship. It's forgiving when someone's mistake hurt your farm or family. It's helping another farmer out when he's in a tight pinch. Or being friendly and helping someone passing through. It's all of this and much, much more. It's following Jesus. It would be a better world if just a few would stop talking Christianity, and start in on a day's work." Floyd sat down, and you could hear a pin drop.

A power capsule
inspired by John 3:16-17

For God so loved the world that he gave his one and only Son, that whoever believes in him shall not perish but have eternal life. For God did not send his Son into the world to condemn the world, but to save the world through him.

God created all mankind – Jesus Christ died for all mankind And God has a wonderful plan for each life!

There is something beautiful in every person!

(If you can't see it – then you have a problem!)

They all stood to sing, *Wonderful Grace of Jesus*, and, for his sermon that morning, Floyd shared the story of the thief on the cross. Several families came to the altar that day, along with a bunch of young men who had played on the New Meadows football team.

Floyd believed in what he said and spent much of his time going from farm to farm to visit people who had never come to church and who probably never would. He was often met by a farm dog and an owner with a shotgun pointed at him. If they had a "still" he would tell them that this wasn't what he was interested in, he just wanted to tell them if they ever needed a pastor or a friend, he would be there. The shotguns would often be put aside, and they would share coffee together. They could tell that he was a man who meant what he said. Very few men could talk like that while looking down the barrel of a shotgun.

One day after doing a funeral, Floyd asked someone from the community about four unmarked graves in the corner of the cemetery. The community leader explained that he didn't know exactly where those graves had come from, except for the fact that someone had come in and buried them in the night over a period of two years. There were a total of four unmarked graves, all located in the same area. Floyd walked over toward the graves, and noticed that this section of the cemetery was different. There was no grass, trees or flowers. As he stood there, he noticed that one of the graves was that of a baby, and two of them were children. Then he remembered visiting one mountain farmer way back in the hills. Upon entering his orchard, the old man had shot two rounds of rock salt at him, and Floyd had turned around and ran. It wasn't a proud moment for the cowboy pastor.

Floyd asked around town, and everyone agreed that this particular farmer was crazy. He lived back in the hills by himself and didn't even come out for supplies. He shot at anyone who would dare to step on his property. It was getting toward evening, and Floyd went home to eat. As they ate, Floyd hardly touched his food, and didn't have a word to say. "What's the matter, Floyd, are you sick? Floyd, do you hear me?" Ione said. He just sat there, staring off into space. She raised her voice, "Floyd, you're frowning."

"I'm sorry, honey," he said, "I've got a hunch I'll be back late."

"A hunch about what?" she asked, but Floyd didn't hear her.

It was just about dark, but Floyd couldn't wait any longer. He had a sense of how that isolated man felt. He mumbled under his breath, "Something has to be wrong for a man to choose to be like that." The shadow of the mountain was cast over the unkempt orchard of this mountain farm. Floyd remembered the storekeeper's rumor: "That man is a killer, and he buries the bodies in the cemetery." As Floyd got out of his car and began the walk through the orchard, fruit bats swooped through the trees. As he approached the old shack, a shot rang out and he jumped. "Get out of here or I'll shoot you," a voice called out.

"I'm Reverend White from New Meadows Methodist Church." Bang, another shot was fired into the air. This time Floyd never flinched. He looked up into a face with blackened teeth, greasy, unkempt hair, and a long beard.

"What do you want, Parson?" The man spat out the words.

The pastor ignored the anger and said, "I want to visit with you. Do you have a cup of coffee?"

"I can't stand churches and Christians, and I don't believe in God. And if you want my opinion of preachers...!" The bitterness just fumed from the man. "Now get out of here before I fill your rear end with rock salt," he yelled.

"Well, you're going to have to shoot me, because I'm not leaving until I get a cup of coffee. I know someone who is lonely and hurting when I see them, because I know what it feels like, and it's hell. You need a friend, and I'm going to be your friend," the minister preached. Floyd's words cut to the heart, and the man's eyes became moist as he said, "A cup of coffee sounds pretty good, I'll put on a pot."

The story came out. The man had lost his wife, son, daughter, and baby to sickness. He had endured it all alone and had become a recluse. The following Sunday at church, many eyes were moist when this lonely mountain farmer walked in and took a seat in the back. He even visited the parsonage for dinner several times. The townspeople became quite friendly to him, and he slowly found a faith in Christ, and became a valued member of the community.

Those were wonderful years for Floyd and Ione in New Meadows with their three boys. Ione felt that they were the best of their whole life. Floyd returned to the town 50 years later. Most of his congregation was gone, but he stopped to talk to a young man sitting on a porch who looked familiar. He called him by name and the young man said gently, "No, old-timer, that's not my name, but that was my dad's name. Now he is in heaven."

Floyd said, "Well, young man, I was your dad's football coach and pastor."

The young man suddenly became very enthusiastic as he said, "Is that right? Then you must have been Reverend White."

Floyd replied with a laugh, "I still am." The man yelled to his wife and kids and introduced them to Floyd. As they sat on the porch drinking sun tea the young man spoke to his child sitting on his lap, "This is the Reverend White who helped Grandpa become a Christian. And he's part of the reason why we're Christians and why your mom and I are happily married and our family has stuck together through hard years. It's because of Christ and the way he worked through this man." The little girl looked at Floyd with respect and wonder in her eyes.

Years later Floyd told his grandson, "What a wonderful thing it is to serve people in the name of Jesus Christ and to share his Good News. More wonderful than you can ever imagine!"

A prayer by Rev. Floyd E. White in a devotional that he wrote about the church in New Meadows entitled "The Mountain Is Still There:"

Thank you, our gracious father, for your blessings that reach beyond the generations. We think of the granite mountain that towers over New Meadows Valley. That mountain has been there towering over the Indians who camped unmolested, on the banks of the Little Salmon River. It was there when the settlers arrived, with visions of making this their homeland and a place to rear their families. Now as Ione and I returned after 50 years, we came through the huge forest trees, rounded the bend in the road, and we looked down on peaceful New Meadows Valley. There was our parish, spread across the lovely landscape. We saw the homes, cattle, hay, and the streams meandering their way toward the big Salmon River. We caught the gleam on the spire of the Church, our Church! This was our Parish, where two of our sons were born. Everything looked the same and the Mountain was still there demonstrating that you are a God that crosses the generations and is always there to respond to our every call. You complete work that we as mortals only begin.

Amen and Amen.

CHAPTER EIGHT

Tough Times, Tough People, and Their Pastor

U.S. hit by dust storm

APRIL 11, 1935

Increasingly severe dust storms are hanging like a black scourge over about half of the United States, destroying millions of dollars worth of wheat crops, forcing untold numbers of people to flee from their farm homes as from a plague, and completely paralyzing all activity in some districts.

The brunt of today's storm fell on western Kansas, eastern Colorado, Wyoming, western Oklahoma, nearly all of Texas, and parts of New Mexico. Breathing was not only difficult but dangerous. While human beings could protect themselves with masks of every sort, all livestock suffered miserably. Dust pneumonia is rapidly increasing among children. And the crop damage is staggering in this, the "nation's breadbasket."

Little relief is in sight, as dust piles up inside houses, schools and businesses are closed, traffic is stopped and bereaved families are unable to bury their dead. In Texas, even the birds are afraid to fly.

Chronicle of the 20th Century, Chronicle Publications, Mount Kisco, New York, 1987, page 443

Tough Times, Tough People, and Their Pastor

"I have held fortune prostrate at my feet
And though beyond the moon was my soaring hope;
Yet, great Quixote, do I still envy thee."

CERVANTES, *The Ingenious Gentleman*
Don Quixote De La Mancha

The year of 1929 was a tough year throughout the world. It was the beginning of the Great Depression, and a time of deep despair. National statistics revealed that unemployment may have risen to 25 percent. Families with children slept in tarpaper shacks and searched for food in city dumps. Thousands of homeless children were on their own after the breakup of their families. Hunger marchers protested bitterly in New York and Chicago. In some parts of the nation, unrest flared into violence. Farmers actually hijacked milk trucks along roads and poured the milk into the ditch. Mobs rioted at farm mortgage sales and ran the bankers out of town.

Arthur M. Schlesinger, Jr., described these events in his book, *The Crisis of the Old Order.*

In January of 1929 Edward A. O'Neil, head of the Farm Bureau Federation, bluntly warned a Senate committee, "Unless something is done for the American farmer, we will have revolution in the countryside within less than 12 months." Senator Hugo Black testified before Congress that it was his expert opinion that class war was ready to erupt. It was the bankruptcy of a nation. Bankruptcy economically and politically as far as having creative answers; and it was bankruptcy religiously as the role of religion in America had to be largely redefined.

Many people who had moved to Oregon and Idaho at this time came from the Dust Bowl. They had come to claim the land, and they themselves represented stories of incredible human hardship. The White boys still remember visiting some of these families with their dad. These people often lived in dugouts with dirt floors, and everything about them depicted poverty and hardship: Their weathered skin, wrinkled hands, and sun-bleached hair were all proof of the struggles and deprivations they had undergone.

As they immigrated into the valley, the Whites could remember such people driving into town with nothing to their name except maybe a prize rocking chair tied to the top of an old broken-down car. The rocking chair itself would tell something of the dramatic hardship and loss they had experienced, and of better days now gone through painful human tragedy.

These people had lost their dreams, many had lost babies, a few came into town missing fathers who had run away, committed suicide, or just chosen to die. There were even single moms and children coming to cut farms out of the dry sagebrush land of Oregon.

On Sundays they came to church. As Floyd explained it, he had no choice but to deliver encouraging sermons on Sundays. These people did not need what little faith they had left torn down Sunday morning. In his classic novel, *The Grapes of Wrath*, author John Steinbeck described these same people.

"Men stood by their fences and looked at the ruined corn, drying fast now, only a little green showing through the film of dust. The men were silent and they did not move often. And the women came out of the houses to stand beside their men — to feel whether this time the men would break. The women studied the men's faces secretly, for the corn could go as long as something else remained. The children stood nearby, drawing figures in the dust with bare toes, and the children sent exploring senses out to see whether the men and women would break. Then they asked, 'What'll we do?' And the men replied, 'I don't know.' But it was all right. The women knew it was all right, and the watching children knew it was all right. Women and children knew deep in themselves that no misfortune was too great to bear if their men were whole."

Floyd and Ione treated these people with dignity. They had their own heartaches, but they did their best to stir new dreams for others. As Floyd took the pulpit, he looked out on a congregation of people who were now clearing the land with not much more than their bare hands. His heart would be greatly moved, as he shared practical messages of faith, which would help these families make it through another week. Many people testified that they barely stretched through a week until they could come back Sunday to get a lift to help them make it through another week. Through the years he watched many children reap the benefits of their parents' tough faith.

During these Depression years, Floyd and Ione, like most ministers, moved quite a bit. The churches where they served throughout their life ministry were: (1) New Meadows, Idaho; (2) Nyssa, Oregon; (3) Apple Valley, Idaho; (4) Ontario, Oregon; (5) Union, Oregon; (6) Cove, Oregon; (7) La Grande, Oregon; (8) Rigdon, Indiana; (9) Point Isabel, Indiana; (10) Vale, Oregon; (11) Joseph, Oregon; (12) Flora, Oregon; (13) Paul, Idaho; (14) Kahlotus, Washington; and (15) Kennewick, Washington.

The Methodist Church in Ontario, Oregon, was perhaps a perfect representation of the church of this time, as it was a basement church — a basement without a building above it. It is still there today, although it is no longer a church.

It was during this time of ministry to these small country towns that Floyd and Ione raised their family. They had six boys: Allen, Jim, John, Dale, Stan, and Edsel. There were often at least two other boys staying with them for one reason or another, which would be a total of eight boys in the White family household.

Not only did Ione have to put up with six boys and poverty, she also had to meet the demands of being a pastor's wife. If that wasn't enough, she worked as a schoolteacher to help support the family, and also served as an ordained minister for country churches that could not afford a full-time pastor. In this situation, both Floyd and Ione were required to grow in character and faith.

These were hard days, and each boy grew up with a bitter taste for poverty. They were never told that poverty had been a choice that Floyd had made. In these years the family was particularly close to Ione's family. In fact, the Fees, Floyd's parents, and sisters were a big help to the struggling minister's family.

Even with all Floyd and Ione's imperfections, the boys knew that wherever they lived, people loved their mom and dad. Floyd and Ione were far from perfect, but they cared deeply for people. They cared year in and year out, and people loved them for that. They could not help but respect their parents for their family's purpose during these hard days. Although times were tough, they were a close family. The kids at school learned quickly to never make fun of a White boy's patched clothes; there were six of them, and they would take on the whole school if they had to. There were many hobos in those days, and the boys got used to having at least one eating at their dinner table each day. There seemed a constant stream of people coming to the parsonage for the food given out in the name of Christ.

The migrant farmers from the Midwest were generally a good-natured people. One day as Floyd drove through the dust ruts to perform a home wedding, the visibility became almost zero. The settlers on the Owyhe Irrigation Project in eastern Oregon were faced with many difficult situations and one of the worst was the terrible dust storms. The wind would sweep down the rolling sand hills, picking up momentum as it tore across the recently cleared sagebrush land. As he neared the house, which had been hastily and loosely constructed, he had to be especially careful that he did not run into a car or truck parked in the yard.

Floyd knocked loudly on the door to be heard above the wind, and the bride welcomed him. They had difficulty in communicating as they made final preparation for the service. Floyd looked around in the dust-filled room and distinguished a number of people seated on one side of the one-room shack. At the kitchen end, a large table had been prepared for the wedding feast. It was covered with several tablecloths and a large blanket was tied over the entire table to keep out the dust that was sifting through the loose boards and around the window and door.

It was decided to wait for an hour and perhaps the wind would die down, but the uproar became even louder. As they sat and waited, the bride's lovely white dress became gray, as it gradually became covered with dust. Floyd's dark blue suit became a light color. Finally the bride made the decision to go ahead with the wedding, and Floyd stood about a foot and a half from the couple. He had to shout to make himself heard, and the guests were unable to distinguish all the words of the ritual. After the ceremony and congratulations were over, the table was unwrapped, but the dirt had even penetrated to the feast. There was much merriment and laughter, as each person blew the dust from the fried chicken, cakes, pies, and other foods.

As Floyd drove home, he thought of all the beautiful weddings he had officiated at, and he thanked God for each opportunity to be there, to ask for God's blessing on those marriages. It was a privilege to tell them that love and loyalty alone will prevail as the foundation of a happy and enduring home. The love of this couple made this wedding one of the most beautiful in his whole ministry. Their hardship highlighted their commitment to each other, just as black velvet can highlight the beautiful glittering light of a diamond.

Hardship and difficulty were like that, and Floyd began to see that he was very fortunate to serve during such tough times. Each time someone came to him with a heartache or a crushed life, he would say a word of thanks because sharing faith in situations like that was an awesome privilege…it was like giving someone a chilled glass of water on a scorching hot day.

More than once there were calamitous natural disasters. Stories of sliding hillsides blocking life-giving irrigation, terrible wind-storms and devastating floods all ran together as Floyd and Ione told me of their Depression days. One drought in particular stood out that illustrated their role during these trials. The drought was annihilating the crops, which were the last chance for most of the migrant farmers. Floyd talked to the county farming engineer and was told how long they would have until the crops would die. Floyd announced in worship that Sunday they were going to God in prayer over the problem.

"Heavenly Father, I've been following you for a long time now, and you've blessed me greatly, and in all those times I haven't asked for much. I haven't really needed to, as you've been so good. Now these good families over whom you have appointed me as a shepherd are hard-working people. They might lose everything for a second time in their lives. We do believe that you know best even when we can't understand. But you have told us in your Holy Word that it is our privilege to ask. Well, we are asking humbly for rain. You are the Almighty —- you intervene in the natural course of things sometimes. I've seen you do it before, do it again — do it now! I believe in you, you know we love you and will follow you no matter what, but bless us now with rain. Lord, these people have worked very hard and bet their lives on their crops. Now I feel like it's my turn to do my work as their pastor, I'm going to stay at this church praying until the rain comes! And I believe it will come. Amen and Amen."

During the prayer, his boys looked around the church in fear at what they were hearing. His son Dale thought, "Oh no, now what has Dad done?" The boys thought about how much they were going to be heckled at school over this preposterous prayer. Then they thought about their dad and how this could just break the back of his ministry; he could be run out of town if it didn't rain. The next morning, Dale slipped into the church to see his father still at the altar praying. His big hands were folded, his head was down, and he was on his knees. Dale quietly slipped out and walked to grade school.

On one such prayer vigil in response to a natural disaster, a county engineer stepped into the church to talk some sense into this naive pastor. "Reverend, what's the matter with you? You're not in your right mind. What are you doing?" He continued, "I believe in God as much as the next man, but if this doesn't work, you'll be remembered as a fool. All the anger they have over their failed crops will be directed toward you."

Floyd thought about those hard words for a long time. When finally he was through thinking, he cleared his throat and replied with such sincerity that the engineer felt his commitment. "I'm not a Holy Roller as you know, but I do believe in doing the right thing, and this is the right thing. It might not make much horse sense to you, but I believe in prayer. I don't believe we make God do what we want, and I've sat with people through enough unexplainable tragedies that I know there is a lot we don't understand. Sure, these people will go through some anger and if it is directed at me rather than them, then that is all right. I'll just continue to be their friend until we work it out. But I'm a pastor, and it's my job to pray in times like this. If I could haul enough water to help their crops I would. Since you asked, let me return the question. What is a farmer going to do without faith when he is struggling to raise his family in not much more than a shack? How will they survive if they lose their dreams? Or if they stop believing the idea that God can and will help them? How can farmers plant seeds in unfriendly soil if they have lost their faith? Some of these people have a list of hurts in their past a mile long. You tell me, how do they make it a month, a week, a day without faith? If they lose their faith they will break. Then they truly will have lost everything."

The preacher continued his personalized sermon. "Tell me, mister, what will happen to the children if these brave people break? I'll tell you what will happen, because I've witnessed it many times. The fathers or mothers will turn to drink and run off and leave them, or they will kill themselves or just choose to give up and die. If this hardship breaks them they have nothing, and nowhere to turn. They have nothing but faith, and when they lose that they have nothing. Before God Almighty, as long as I have strength and faith and love, I just won't let that happen. Not to my flock, not in my lifetime!"

The emotion was easy to detect in his voice as he said, "I know what it's like to give into such faithless thoughts and as long as I follow the good Lord Jesus, we will do whatever it takes to fight those thoughts with faith. Even if it backfires on me. In the long run every one of them will know that someone cares. God cared for me, and I can do no less!"

Both men were quiet for a minute, as the sound of the preacher's impromptu sermon disappeared in the empty church. Then the engineer, who had followed the homespun logic replied, "Well, when you explain it that way, I guess the only one it can hurt is you, and that's your privilege."

On the way home from school, Dale was worried, and thought, "I've got to have a long talk with Dad." Just as he said that to himself, he felt something wet hit his head and looked up to see the rain falling. He began to run for the church. He was filled with the warmth of faith, and the joy he experienced was as though he had witnessed a barnburner of a basketball game with his very own dad hitting the winning basket at the last second! As he ran, he heard the church bells ring. When Dale reached the church he saw people coming from all over to give thanks to the Almighty God. One of the people running into the church was the county engineer.

Floyd loved to whistle the great hymns and Ione hated it. So Floyd whistled under his breath when he was happy. He was whistling most of the time. But when he was really sad, he sang, and Ione or no Ione, he would sing at the top of his lungs when he was discouraged. The family would hear him, and they would leave him alone with his Lord. But he never could remember the words to any songs and that drove them all crazy. Nevertheless, it wouldn't be too long until he would be whistling again, and they knew that God had done his work.

One day in Vale, Oregon, Floyd was working on the parsonage when it caught fire. The fire spread quickly. He yelled to Ione, and they grabbed the boys and made it out of the house as the flames came through the roof. They huddled outside against the cold wind, watching the volunteers fight the fire. The children moved closer to their parents and studied their faces to see if they would break. The neighboring farmers were about to give up on fighting the fire and they also stole glances at their pastor to see his reaction to this tragic event.

Floyd turned to Ione and said, "Well, we hardly had anything and God is taking that away." Ione looked back and her eyes twinkled as they had on the train ride when he had asked her name. She felt like it was again her turn to give her husband a hint as to her identity. "We've got everything that really matters here, Floyd," she replied. Floyd looked a little more hopeful, but he was angry and depressed. In utter frustration he yelled, "What is the church going to say when they find out I burned down their parsonage?"

The family watched as he walked over to the incinerated parsonage looking for something to salvage, and they saw him blackened by the smoke and the charcoal. They listened as he sang, and it was off key as usual. But they were amazed, because he remembered the words. His voice was full of emotion as he sang.

Abide with me; fast falls the eventide,
Earth's joys grow dim, its glories pass away,
When other helpers fail, and comforts flee,
Help of the helpless, O, abide with me.

A power capsule
inspired by John 14:27

Peace I leave with you; my peace I give you.
I do not give to you as the world gives;
Do not let your heart by troubled and do not be afraid.

Let go and let God!

(Jesus said, "Come unto me all you who are burdened
and heavy laden and I will give you rest!")

A few of the volunteer firemen laughed and made jokes about the bad singing, but the family looked on with amazement and respect.

I fear no foe, with Thee at hand to bless;
Ills have no weight, and tears no bitterness.
Who like Thy-self, my guide and stay can be?
I triumph still, If Thou abide with me.

A lady from the church walked up to the soot-covered pastor. "Thank you, Reverend White," she said.

He glanced up. "For what?" he asked.

"For doing in 20 minutes what we've needed to do for 20 years," she replied with faith. There was a big crowd there by then, and they all agreed. She went on to explain. "We've needed to build a new parsonage for a long time. Now we will have to do what we should have wanted to do." And the people began to bring things for this pastor's family who they loved. The following weeks were some of the best of their lives, as they lived in the biggest house in town…the church.

The times were tough, but they brought the community together. The shortcomings were apparent, and people really needed to care for one another to get through those times. Although the Depression meant hunger and hard times, it also meant common dedication to an end larger than self or profit. In such times a society can be reborn.

Just as there were droughts and problems with the economy, there were other crises on the horizon. One day Floyd and Ione drove out to look at the rising waters of Bully Creek where it enters the Malheur River. A 24-hour rain had combined with the melting of the heavy snow pack above Juntura, and had brought down water in torrents. They were not really alarmed, and when they got home they decided to walk down to the river bridge. Before they had traveled very far, they realized they should turn back as someone in a truck shouted that the flood was really coming.

The storeowners were working to secure windows and doors, and the water was swirling through the streets. By the time they reached their house, they were wading waist deep and they crawled up on the porch, numb from the icy bath.

Soon trucks were coming down the street to evacuate the residents. Floyd and Ione decided to stay, as they could not foresee any great danger, but it wasn't long before they wished they had evacuated. Later, they watched as water filled the stairwell of the church basement. It was a fearful night as Floyd kept measuring the water as it came up and onto the porch. Ione was glad that she had insisted that the younger boys leave with people from the church. About midnight they heard a great crashing and shaking of the house, and realized that the flood had forced down a basement wall. The clanking and bumping of jars and other things followed the sound. Ione remarked, "There goes the canned fruit!"

When the door was broken open they could hear the agonizing bawling of drowning cattle as they were swept down stream. The water stopped rising about four o'clock in the morning, and the family went to bed upstairs for a couple of hours. They woke the next morning to the sound of a small motorboat chugging down the street. It was the postmaster on his way to the post office to try to salvage the mail. Floyd waded across the yard to the church and peered into the basement, where he saw the piano floating like a battleship.

The town clean-up was a major task. Neighbor helped neighbor and many came from other towns to help. The people of the entire area received typhoid shots and the White family boiled their drinking water for weeks. For several Sundays the churches of Union, Oregon, held services together. They ran an ad in the paper saying, "We are not just back in business, and we have never been out of business."

In those tough times, Floyd's reputation spread throughout the valley. If you were really in trouble, you could be sure he would do everything he could to help. One day as Floyd was studying in his office, one of his boys came running. "Mom wants you at the house." As Floyd arrived in his living room he saw a thin little tyke huddled close to a woman sitting tensely in a chair, and whimpered, "I'm hungry, Mama." The father stood uneasily twisting his hat in his hands, and the mother spoke softly to the child, who soon became quiet. Because of their experience dealing with people who came to the parsonage during those Depression days seeking assistance, Floyd and Ione felt they were becoming able to separate real needs from panhandling needs. The stories usually were similar, but then almost everyone had financial troubles in the early thirties. Floyd and Ione found that they were moved to compassion by this young, weary, depressed couple and their little girl, more than they had been in some time. Their old car was out of gas and oil, and a tire was beyond repair. They asked for help to take them over the Blue Mountains and on to Yakima, where they had been promised work.

The little one cried plaintively and the mother tried to soothe her, but the child replied, "Am too! Am too!" Ione asked if they had eaten any lunch and they answered that the little tot had had a few crackers for her breakfast. Again the child burst forth in a piping voice, "I'm hungry, Mama." Ione fixed the family a beautiful lunch, much more than she ever prepared for her own family. After lunch she handed them some towels and soap and a suggestion that the little one be given a bath. As Ione packed a dinner for them to take with them, the boys watched in amazement, for half of that was their own dinner. Floyd tried to explain that this was all they could do and they did not have the cash for the gas, oil, and a new tire. Ione gave him one of those smiles after which she gave the boys a sharp look to keep them in check about giving away their dinner.

Floyd told the man to go down to the filling station, "Tell the man to charge the gas, oil, and tire to me."

The couple asked together, "How do you know if we'll ever be able to pay you back?"

Ione interrupted, "You're starting a new life, and things will work out for you this time. We believe in you." As they walked out of the yard, Ione turned to Floyd, and said the same thing she had said when they left for the ministry in New Meadows, "God will provide."

After several months, they received a well-written letter from the family with one dollar enclosed. Over the period of a year or more they received a little money at a time until the tire, gas, and oil had been paid for. Each time they wrote saying, "Thanks for believing in us even when we couldn't!"

A doorbell ringing any hour of the day or night at the parsonage was not unusual. Early one Monday morning, just as Floyd was hoping for a little extra rest to recuperate from a strenuous Sunday, an insistent bell awakened him. When he opened the door he was greeted with a brisk and cheery, "Good morning, Reverend, may I come in? I have a very unusual request."

The man's clothing was clean, though wrinkled and threadbare. When they were seated, his first words were startling. "May I borrow your white shirt and tie from you?" he asked in a straightforward manner. Floyd got many requests, but none was more unusual than this one. Floyd heard Ione making coffee in the kitchen, so he suggested the man tell his story while they waited for breakfast.

They had heard many hard luck stories over the past several years, and Floyd was a bit skeptical, but he took note of the stranger's clear eyes and cultured speech. He was a scientist from an eastern state and had applied for a position with the new sugar company in town. He had been asked to come to town for an interview, but he had been without work for sometime, and therefore could not raise the bus fare for an interview. Those were desperate days in the 1930s, and he started out for the far west by hitchhiking and walking. By pushing his luck he arrived the evening before his appointment. The sheriff gave him a place to sleep in the city jail, and he had been able to shower and shave there. The sheriff then suggested he go to the parsonage for help with his problem of a clean shirt.

When the story was finished, breakfast was ready. This was the first real meal the man had eaten since leaving the East. While they were eating, Ione brought out Floyd's only white shirt from his meager wardrobe.

Wearing Floyd's shirt, the early breakfast guest disappeared down the street toward the sugar mill. Floyd turned to Ione, "I have to confess, I think that's the last time I'll see that shirt." Ione smiled, "O, ye of little faith!" Floyd went on, "Only about half the people we help have proven worthy or at least returned to say 'thank you.'"

One boy who was watching asked, "Dad that's your only Sunday shirt. What are you going to do next week, wear a wool work shirt under your robe?"

Floyd patted him on the head. "Well, the Lord has one week to provide."

About three o'clock in the afternoon, as Floyd was mowing the back lawn, one of the boys stuck his head over the fence. "Dad, the shirt man is coming this way and he's smiling."

The man's first words were, "Oh, Reverend, I do thank you! I have the position for certain, and it is partly because of the breakfast and the clean shirt!" They saw the man in church often and he stayed with the local company until he was transferred to another state. The boys always called him *the shirt man*, and yes, Floyd got his shirt back, and eventually a new one as a "thank you gift." But more then that, Floyd's faith was greatly enhanced by his encounter with what he called *a diamond in the rough!*

While those were tough times, they were good times too. When the boys get together and remember them, they often laugh so hard that they can hardly sit up. Six boys can cause much mischief in a small community. In one town where they lived, the church was also used as a funeral home for the community. The kids of the town were convinced this old place was haunted. They "knew" bodies were stored in the basement and cobwebs grew there because of it was seldom used. When the Whites moved to town, the town's people began to notice that noises started to come from the old building. One day as Floyd was walking down the street with a neighbor kid, the kid started to walk across the street before they reached the church/funeral home. Floyd asked, "What's the matter?"

The boy was shaking as he replied, "That place is haunted, Reverend, and your boys are either vampires or they are in league with ghosts, because they go there."

Floyd walked up to the old building and heard a loud crash. When he found a window to look into the basement, he heard a sound like thunder. Coming down a ramp from upstairs into the basement were four of his boys, zooming down the ramp in a casket perched on a table with wheels.

Slowly but surely, everyone in the family accepted the fact that theirs was a family with a unique calling. When Floyd would rush out on one emergency after another, the boys understood. They were proud to be "preacher's kids." Even if they did defy the image sometimes.

To describe only the difficulties of those days would be to do them an injustice. One story the family can hardly talk about without falling off their chairs in laughter is the one of a lady in a nearby town who always felt she was one notch above the rest of the people who lived in the valley. She was wealthy and arrogant, and because of her high social position she always felt she was the only cultured one in the valley. That was all right, but there were many struggling young mothers who were sent home in tears because of the artful put-downs by this lady. Most people realized all this highfalutin hog wash was because this extremely heavyset lady must have had a problem with her own feelings of self-dignity. Because of this, she never missed church even if her cultural exclusiveness did more to cause divisions in the church and the town than anything else did.

These people needed the fellowship of quilting bees and potluck dinners more during these times than any other time. The church people knew the lady would have to come down a notch and at the same time learn that the rest of the town accepted her.

One Sunday their prayers were answered in a way that proved God has a sense of humor. In fact, the whole valley had the privilege of enjoying God's creative answer to this dilemma. For those who don't remember the days of the outhouse, you need to know the unique social importance of this sociological phenomenon. It was the great leveler of social distinction, because using an outhouse was a terrible and humiliating experience. Not only did it stink in a way that cannot be adequately described, but there was virtually no privacy to this humbling experience. Everyone knew when a person was in the outhouse, and exactly what he or she was up to. You just did not use an outhouse to powder your nose. The great social aspect of this phenomenon was that everyone had to use the same outhouse. Rich and poor, king and peasant, saint and sinner, all were humiliated at one time or another every day. It just came down to the fact that there was not a dignified way to use an outhouse.

On this particular Sunday, the heavyset lady with all the social prestige slipped out of the service to use the outhouse outside the church. Unfortunately, while humans hated outhouses, carpenter ants loved them. And this particular outhouse must have been supremely tasty to the carpenter ants, because they had virtually devoured the strength from the wood of this particular outhouse. No one heard the first cracking, but the seat gave way when this socialite was sitting in a very undignified position. She became stuck in this unromantic place and could not free herself from the seat. Somehow she summoned the ushers and as privately and discreetly as possible, they tried to free her. She was very thankful for their efforts, as she was (shall we say) hanging by not much more than a thread over a fate worse than death. As thankful as she was for their discreet efforts, sometimes bad things happen to good people, and this was one of those times. The whole seat collapsed and she ended up, shall we say, six feet under. The high soprano cries of the socialite interrupted the service and the whole church came to help. One after another, they struggled to free her from this devastating dilemma, and they did it with a straight face. But the physical bounty of this woman was just too much, so they had to call the fire department. Now the whole town was involved, and it took a team of horses to pull her out. Needless to say, it is just impossible to think you are better than anyone else after spending Sunday morning at the center of such a community event.

The duties of a pastor were varied in those days, just as they are today. As Floyd walked down the hospital corridor with Harvey's wife and mother, he suggested they ask for consultation for Harvey, because he felt he was not doing well. They agreed his strength was failing. They left Floyd with the promise that they would call Floyd and report the doctor's findings. At six o'clock the next morning, Floyd was called to the hospital and was told Harvey had only a few hours to live. His wife and mother asked that Floyd tell him this news, as they could not bring themselves to do so. Floyd knew Harvey was not spiritually ready to die. He didn't have much time to share with Harvey the plan of salvation and other spiritual truths, which would help him to face the coming challenge. Harvey whispered to Floyd that he accepted Christ as his Savior and wanted to be baptized. Floyd ministered the rites of Baptism there in the hospital room with the nurse's assistance. Then, gathering his waning strength, Harvey talked quietly with his wife for a short time. She told Floyd that Harvey's last wish was that she also would become a follower of Christ. Kneeling by the side of his bed, with her hand in his, she dedicated herself to the Christian way of life.

Floyd had other urgent appointments and had to go. He told Harvey he would be back as soon as possible. "If the Lord calls you home before I get back are you ready to meet Him, Harvey?"

"Yes," was the faint whisper, "I'm ready, Reverend White." When Floyd returned, he met Harvey's wife and mother descending the hospital stairs and knew Harvey was gone. They told him Harvey had passed to the great beyond in perfect peace.

As Floyd returned to the church, he thought about his good feelings about being there for people. It always seems people die, are born, get married, and go through hardship at the most inconvenient times. Every time the Whites prepared to go fishing or to take a break, you could be sure some emergency was going to happen. The call to ministry was a family call.

On their vacation they would sometimes travel outside the area to pick fruit with other migrant workers. They would do this so they would not embarrass the good people of their church with the fact they were not giving them enough money to get by. But according to Floyd and Ione, even in those times the boys made the best of it, and they were always good boys. The way the boys tell the story, they were so good on those long trips even when they traveled from Oregon to Indiana because Floyd had the uncanny ability to be able to spank six boys in the back seat while driving full speed down the road! As Ione tells it, the boys were good because they loved the trips and they would all find girlfriends on every one of their fruit-picking trips.

Through these years the communities that Floyd and Ione worked in held great admiration for them. In fact, one Catholic bank president called Floyd into his bank and informed the Methodist minister that he did not make enough to live on and that he was one of the poorest people in the valley. The banker said, "With all you do for the people in this valley, you are a community resource!" He went on to say, "I've been watching you for years — you come into my bank anytime you want and I'll tell the tellers to give you the amount of money you need to take care of your family. You name your salary and I'll pay it!"

Floyd thought for a moment then said, "No, I can't take it, even if you are a fellow Mason. It would make my church feel terrible to think that they couldn't pay me enough. It wouldn't be right. I wouldn't have to trust the Lord anymore."

The banker said, "You're a man of integrity, Reverend White — one of a kind."

Floyd replied, "I'm afraid you're wrong, pastors have been living on faith for almost 2,000 years — and there are thousands in the United States alone. God takes care of us through the tithes of the good people in our church; and you ought to be tithing to your church."

The banker said, "Well I've never known a man to turn down a guaranteed salary." For Floyd and Ione, that was just another sign from God telling them what they already knew by now: God would provide for all their needs.

The Whites did a lot of fishing and hunting together in the mountains of Oregon and Idaho. It didn't hurt the youth group to have six boys, either. In more than one of their churches, the number of youth rose to over a hundred.

At one parsonage, the bathroom caused quite a difficulty for the six boys and all of their guests. The older boys soon found that if they violently shook the door, the lock would slowly rattle its way open.

One day, Jim thought Dale or Edsel was in the bathroom when he demanded they open the door, so he began to shake the door violently. Each time he would stop and listen to nothing but deathly silence. In a couple of minutes he broke into the bathroom to find the district superintendent (their dad's boss) in a very unreligious position. The look on his face — well it can best be described as not the confident, commanding look of an executive minister. The whole family blamed Jim when they were moved to a new church.

There were occasions when Floyd was clearly reminded of God's power and ability to answer prayers during times of tragic events. Floyd arrived at the hospital just as the ambulance pulled up to the emergency entrance. He felt a little embarrassed at breaking the speed limit after the telephone call came telling him of Bill's accident. It was after midnight when two young men living near the railroad switchyards heard an anguished cry for help. They found Bill by the side of the tracks, in a terrible condition. He had been working at his job as brakeman when the accident occurred; and he was never able to remember the details. A young railroad man administered first aid, while the other one summoned the ambulance and called Floyd. Bill was receiving a transfusion and blood was flowing even now from his partly severed legs. Floyd spoke a few words to him and he responded by whispering, "I'm so thankful that I know the Lord. Pray for me, Reverend White." And there, for a brief moment, the doctors and nurses bowed their heads while Floyd asked God's help for this fine team of surgeons. As the doctors continued to work, Floyd gave Bill his medicine, Psalm 46, verse one.

"God is our refuge and strength, a very present help in trouble."

Bill looked at his pastor with a faint smile and closed his eyes as he turned and left the room. Floyd's thoughts went back to the evening in the church, just a few weeks before, when Bill had dedicated his life to Christ. Floyd thanked God for the working of the Holy Spirit. Bill lost both legs but he came through victorious in his faith. On the first Sunday that Bill walked into church with his wooden legs, everyone, no matter how tough their problems, believed in a God that could help them in those problems. When he walked down the aisle and knelt at the altar to receive communion, there was scarcely a dry eye in the sanctuary.

Prayer by Rev. Floyd White at the close of a sermon preached in the days of the Depression:

Our dear Heavenly Father, the one to whom Jesus turned in prayer, teach us how to speak to thee. Educate us to understand thy simple words of love. As youth we open our hearts to thee — show us how to be worthy of thy companionship by letting go of small and petty desires. Wash us clean of prejudice and boastfulness; take away all selfishness that we may stand humbly and purely in thy presence.

Grant that the commandments of love may be written anew in our hearts. May they be our guides as we live our lives in our homes, our schools, and our communities. Show us what it means to be our brother's keeper. May we be ready to accept the challenge of our Christ to "Go ye..." and do our part in spreading the glorious Gospel. Be thou a companion to each of us as we go our ways again. This we pray through Jesus Christ our Lord.

Amen and Amen.

Chapter Nine

Heart Wounds

36,000 taken on Bataan

April 9, 1942

Allied forces, badly outnumbered, sick, and famished, have finally been crushed by the Japanese on the Bataan Peninsula after four months of savage fighting. The Americans and Filipinos, commanded by General Jonathan Wainwright, could not hold out any longer. Nearly all of the 36,000 defenders were killed or captured by an assault force of 200,000 Japanese. Several thousand Marines were apparently able to slip off the tip of Bataan into Manila Bay and escape to Corregidor. The island fortress is still in Allied hands.

Secretary of War Stimson says the Americans put up "a long and gallant defense." They had plenty of ammunition, but were very short on food. The forces had been on half-rations since January and were sharing their supplies with 20,000 civilians who had been evacuated from Luzon. "We have nothing but praise for these men." Stimson said. "I believe it to be a temporary loss. This country, in fulfillment of its pledge, will ultimately drive out the invaders."

Chronicle of the 20th Century, Chronicle Publications,
Mount Kisco, New York, 1987, page 536

Heart Wounds

"Oh, the vain hopes of men! What thing is worse?
Yet do at last in smokes our glories end!"

Dale Wasserman, MAN OF LA MANCHA

December 7, 1941, changed the whole nation and the country people were no exception. Floyd and Ione cried when their son Allen joined the armed forces and was sent into the thick of naval combat. To some degree this was Floyd's fault, and a matter of disagreement in the family.

Floyd was always extremely patriotic. After Pearl Harbor, he encouraged and directed Allen to go into the Navy. As he explained it to me, this may have been one of the greatest mistakes of his life. His distance from all of his boys as they were growing up was a wound he seemingly never noticed as a younger man. But it brought great tears as he shared it with me later in life. As he shared his regrets, he also shared with me how thankful he was that his boys had forgiven him and that they loved him.

The years had passed quickly since Floyd and Ione had fallen in love, married, and experienced the joy at each of their boys' births. The hard and demanding life they led had not allowed them to spend the time they would have liked with each child. Floyd's temper and harsh discipline were regrets he carried and wrestled with for over half a century. Ione's cold, practical demeanor and controlling personality were issues of pain to her as she recalled her story. But beneath it all, there was great love growing as each year passed, and this was sometimes expressed in ambition. For a whole nation, World War II was a time of making mistakes and growing up.

One Sunday afternoon, a handsome young man named Carl brought his lovely young girlfriend to Floyd's study. Floyd thought he had never seen such a fine young couple. Carl had just a few days before he was to be inducted into the Air Force. They were so in love, and after much counseling and talking to the parents, Floyd performed their wedding. The young couple enjoyed a few days of complete happiness and were separated until Carl finished his training. He was home for a short time, and when he and his wife said goodbye, neither one realized it would be two long, agonizing years before they would see each other again. Little did anyone dream of the tragedies they were to face in the next 24 months.

The young wife was very proud of her husband; he was an Army Air Force pilot in a squadron of fighters. For a time their letters were exchanged regularly, but as the war spread over the Pacific, her letters were returned and she had no word of him. When she found out they would have a child, she was unable to share the good news with her husband. Time passed, and on the very day the baby was born, news came that Carl had been shot down in the South Pacific. The next day the doctor told her the baby would not live but a few hours. Floyd was called to the hospital and waited with the mother and grandmother while the tiny spark of life left the precious body.

After returning from the burial service for the baby, Carl's mother and Floyd returned to the hospital. They found the young wife had developed complications that might end her life. At Floyd's suggestion, Carl's mother and grandmother entered into a covenant of prayer with him. They decided on a certain time every day when they would pray for Carl and his wife, and they would leave the answer to the Heavenly Father. Many months passed after that covenant began, and the war came to a close. A friend who came home by way of India reported that he had seen Carl in a city there.

On one beautiful Sunday morning in May, just after the opening prayers in the morning service, people suddenly became aware that Floyd was having trouble speaking and his eyes were moist. At the back of the church stood Carl, his wife and his mother just beaming smiles at him. Floyd stopped and said a prayer of thanksgiving with the entire church. Later, Carl shared his war experiences. He said that as a prisoner of war, he would have starved if it were not for a Japanese guard that he suspected was a Christian. The guard had shared some of his own rations with Carl, risking his own life in doing so. Carl was most impressed when he was released, and the guard returned his wedding ring that had been taken when he was captured. The guard had saved it for him throughout his captivity.

The experiences of being a pastor in rural America during the Second World War made this Army-veteran pastor even more patriotic. Being with families when they heard the news of losing their kids, along with his love and concern for his own boys, gave Floyd a deeper appreciation for freedom and liberty. Floyd was moved by the importance of the church and Sunday school as he watched kids he had personally taught to pray go off to war.

During this period there were also some very great discouragements at home. The church was designed with a very weak pastoral leadership role. In many cases, Methodist churches were more like service organizations: People often treated them like clubs. Therefore, there was an underlying power struggle that was a major discouragement to many pastors, and Floyd was no exception.

He did not have a college degree until later in his life. Although he never completed his seminary education, he spent his life in continuing education. This meant that when it came time to compete for pastoring a church he had built up himself, he was often sent to a smaller church, while a seminary graduate was brought into the new, larger church. This meant perpetual poverty for the Whites and fighting the same battles again somewhere else within the church.

Floyd did not remember the exact cause of one particular political battle in a new church where he had been moved. The power of the church rested with one particular lady. Floyd's good-natured approach and firm determination soon led this lady to believe that she would no longer be able to control the church. One day she walked out of church and announced in front of everyone she was quitting. She then walked over and slapped Floyd in the face in front of the whole church! Floyd pretended he hardly even noticed, but for months he went into a long and deep depression.

Ione finally noticed he was not himself when he lit into one of his boys behind the woodshed, because it had turned from discipline to abuse. She waited until they were alone in his study when she lit into him. Floyd also had a terrible temper and this was one of the worst arguments they ever had. The next day, when they met again in his study, he apologized and said that he did not know what the matter was. He said he was tired of poverty, and he was going to quit the ministry. He had set out to do something really great, but now it was dawning on him he would never do anything like the great preachers he admired, preachers like E. Stanley Jones and Norman Vincent Peale. In fact, he could see himself spending his life in churches that were barely making it, and when he built them up they would have to move to another struggling church.

Ione had never seen him like this before, even through the two parsonage fires or the flood. Floyd was so discouraged he wasn't even singing. She spoke to him as she had when they were deciding to launch their first ministry in New Meadows.

"Floyd," she said, "everything you say is true, but I disagree with the conclusions you are drawing. We will probably always be in these small country churches. And E. Stanley Jones is E. Stanley Jones and Norman Vincent Peale is Norman Vincent Peale and both of us love them and thank the Lord that they are who they are. But if they knew Floyd White, they would be thanking the Lord you are who you are.

"You know I am one of the most honest critics of your preaching, and I will tell you that you are not a great preacher like some of the big city preachers. You have a great voice because it is always full of kindness. Nobody can keep the children's attention through a Bible story like you, but you are just you. Maybe, Floyd, these hard times are here so that both of us will learn that fact."

Floyd said despairingly, "But nobody will ever remember a single sermon I have given, and I work so hard at it."

Ione told him, "The children will remember, Floyd. If nobody else, you have six boys who will remember you as the greatest Bible storyteller in the world. You know that you are the one who has taught so many children to pray, let alone to know that the Almighty loves them." Floyd paused, and a transformation took place before the skillful eyes of Ione.

He stood up and slapped his desk. "Well then, by old Doc Collister, if there is one little Ephraim who is helped in all my years, only one, then it is worth it! Come on, cheap church politics, come on, stacks of firewood that need to be cut and no one notices. Come on, late night calls and wild children's church times. Come on, sermons where people are sleeping because they are worn out, not because the sermon is bad, come one come all, because you're right, Ione, I never bargained for anything more! I may not be much, but I will be my best self for the Glory of God and may every one of my boys be proud of me because each of them knows that I gave it all I had!"

"Now don't get carried away, Floyd!" Ione could dash Floyd from any height or lift him up when nobody else could reach him, but what she said that day worked. The next Sunday Floyd was his old self again in the pulpit. The boys knew he was happy again because he was whistling, and how he whistled when he was happy! He was like a fine musician when he whistled, and everyone loved it, except Ione.

As encouraging as that event was for Floyd, there was an even more encouraging event awaiting him. Dwight was a young man who had grown up in their church, and he had served in the Army Air Force during World War II. Someone neglected to fill the auxiliary tanks of the B-17 that Dwight was on, and one little error cost the lives of several men and a very valuable plane. Distress signals were sent out, but no reply came. Soon after midnight the plane was out of gasoline and the pilot was forced to set it down on the water.

The wounded and non-swimmers were placed in the raft, and the rest hung on and swam alongside. Some of the men were casualties on their way back from the war zone. The commanding officer arranged the men according to their needs, and flares were sent up in an attempt to attract the attention of other planes. Their own plane went under soon after they managed to escape at a safe distance, and they were left alone — afloat on the vast Pacific Ocean in the murky darkness. Their greatest terror came from the man-eating sharks. A number of times a cry of terror would be heard, and in trying to account for each man at given intervals, it was found that another one was missing.

It was a terrible night as the group hung on and swam beside the raft. Some of the critically wounded begged to be thrown off the craft in order to give their places to those swimming in the shark-infested waters. During the night every type of human nature came out. Some cursed God for allowing such a tragedy to occur, while others prayed. Finally one of the men suggested that they pray the *Lord's Prayer*, each taking turns around the raft.

As Dwight related the story to his pastor he said, "I do not know how long the prayer vigil lasted, but I do know that those of us who were left were given courage and strength by that chain of prayer, and that enabled us to hang on until the sun came up and warmed our chilled bodies. Soon a scout plane was sighted and signaled it had located us. Two more planes came over and we were rescued from our terrible plight." That day in Floyd's study, Dwight told him, "I will always firmly believe that the Circle of Prayer saved our lives and our sanity...it may not seem like much here and now but it is...keep teaching children to pray, Reverend."

Moments like that encouraged Floyd and Ione. They knew that doing the little things very well was their calling, and through the years consistency and integrity would become the hallmarks of their ministry.

As Floyd rang the first bell for the Sunday evening service his thoughts were on his sermon. The bigger, more exciting Sunday morning worship was over. For every minister, Sunday evenings are always tough. The crowd is smaller. Some come because they feel they have to, and they can sense that in the service. The music is often a chore, and the minister himself is usually dead tired from a busy day. Floyd thanked the Almighty for his apprenticeship with Dr. Collister. The late night calls, and the little things nobody noticed were all a part of Dr. Collister's life as well. The fatigue was the same whether he was praying with a dying person or operating or delivering a baby. The internship with the old Irish doctor had taught him how to be a pastor because it taught him how to care whether he felt like it or not. Floyd's mind flashed back to the kid in the car crossing the dark stream. "Nobody expects it!" cried Ephraim. "I expect it," answered the Irish doctor. The sound of the turbulent water could still be heard in his imagination.

Floyd had worked hard on his sermon, whether anyone would come or not he would share the encouragement of the Good News with all the strength he could muster. Floyd walked back to the parsonage for a few minutes and soon there was a knock on the door. A nice-looking young woman stood there. Floyd could see at a glance that she was very disturbed. He took the visitor to his study and she unfolded such a sordid story that only a part of it should be told.

She had been working as a housekeeper for a stockman in the interior of the state whose wife was seriously ill. She had gone to her parents' home in Portland, Oregon, and after several weeks, her former employer called on her and asked her to take a ride in his new car. For the next three days they had driven many miles, and both of them had become increasingly intoxicated. She could not remember the details, except that he kept giving her liquor. Then becoming tired of her, he kicked her out of the car on a lonely road in the dark of the night. She walked to town, and secured a room in the hotel. After sobering up, she realized what an awful mess she was in but was afraid and too ashamed to call her parents.

In her despair she decided to go to the river about a quarter of a mile from town, and there to end it all in the depth of the dark waters. She cried out to the lonely countryside, "There's no hope!" Her cries echoed against the hillsides. The loneliness was like a cold blanket covering nature, but as her call echoed out it seemed to bring the sound of the church bell. It was the first call for service. A great urge came upon her, and she walked the opposite direction from the river to the church.

She met Floyd ringing the bells. After he and Ione heard her story and spent some time in council and prayer, they took her to the evening service. During the evening the Holy Spirit spoke to her, and she dedicated her life to Christ at the altar of that Methodist Church. A soul was saved for eternity.

Later in the evening, Ione invited her to the parsonage for a good supper and another long talk. She believed her relatives were looking for her and asked Floyd to call and tell them she was all right.

The next morning Floyd and Ione took her to the river and baptized her there in the name of the Father, and of the Son, and of the Holy Spirit. Thus she found a new spiritual life in the same river where she had planned to end her physical one.

Floyd found her a temporary job, and eventually she moved home to Portland. Years later they received a letter with a picture of her husband and a beautiful family. In the letter of appreciation she spoke of the *Bells of Hope*, which called her to a new life.

Through these years the communities in which Floyd and Ione worked held great admiration for them. In fact, in one community they ran Floyd for the legislature without his approval. He was offered the Democratic Party's backing in this Democratic district. He thought about it, as he had been interested in politics since being president of the student body at Boise High School. After praying about it, he refused the backing of the Democratic Party, even though he had been a dyed-in-the-wool Democrat his whole life. He felt that as a minister he would not be able to represent either party, that he would have to remain independent. He came in second in that election in which he refused to campaign, second to the Democratic contender.

It almost sounds like the story of a saint, and that is how some looked at him. But they were human just as we all are. What I say here about their heart wounds might have been easier if this book was about someone else's grandparents. When Ione and I drove to the convalescent center to see her sister, Grace, as she was dying, Grandma told me she wanted me to be a pastor first. Grace might want to confess some sins to me before she died. When we visited Grace, Grandma told her the same thing and then left us alone in the room. Grace told me how proud my grandparents were that I was a pastor, but she did not need to tell me anything she did not have already clear with Jesus.

When Grandma was dying, they turned me from biographer to priest-confessor, but I was always a grandson whether they were remembering that or not.

Grandpa did tell me about going to visit Edna Simpson in what he called the *poor house* as she was dying. Grandpa called the convalescent centers poor houses, and it was his deepest wish that neither Grandma nor he would have to die in one.

Whether there had ever been a romantic involvement between Grandpa and Edna is open to conjecture, but there is no question about the bitter rivalry between the two. Edna had lost all of her inheritance, and her husband had left her after she lost everything. In fact, Grandpa said it was because they knew nothing about running a ranch. Grandpa tried to share with her the Good News of Jesus Christ, but she chose to die as she had lived, in bitterness.

As Grandpa walked out to his car, he said he was struck by the fact that his inheritance of learning to care for people had paid greater dividends, not only financially, but also in terms of happiness, friends, and family.

Grandma had been hard to live with through those years. She was always unhappy about where they lived. When I asked her why, she said it was because she would have liked to have spent their entire life at New Meadows.

Through all their failings, their boys were always the most important priority to their hearts. Because of the difficulties they had encountered due to their lack of education, it was very important to them that all of their boys graduate from college. John was the only son who did not graduate from college, and in a way, John reminds more people of Grandpa than anyone else. He is always joking around, and as the third son he was one of the spark plugs of the family.

At one time he felt called to the ministry, and at Grandma's urging he went to the altar to confess his calling. This made Grandpa so proud he moved all of his family to Indiana so that John and Jim would have a chance to attend Taylor University, a fine Christian college. The whole family sacrificed for the two boys to go to school. Unfortunately, John just hated college! He would cut classes and go pick up a girl in the family car. Grandpa went without books so his boys could have books. He went without shoes so his boys could have good school shoes. The time that broke John's heart the most was when his dad took a second job at a filling station so they could get enough gas for the boys to go to school.

A power capsule
inspired by Romans 5:20

But where sin increased, grace increased all the more!

There is no hurt on earth that heaven cannot heal!

*(Your weaknesses can become a monument
testifying of God's grace and power!)*

One day as he was driving back home after being out with a girl, he passed his dad, who had been cutting wood for someone, and was carrying a two-man saw. John felt so guilty! To make matters worse, one day during the height of the Korean War, after watching a John Wayne movie he was so inspired he went right over and joined the Marines. The life expectancy of a Marine at that time in Korea was not very long. One of the hardest things John ever did was to open the screen door, walk into the kitchen, and tell his mom and dad he had joined the Marines, without even talking to them first.

John was a steelworker most of his life. While he was in the Marines, he met a girl in Florida and remained there. About a year before Floyd died, the two of them went for a walk. It was a beautiful fall evening with autumn-colored leaves. It was the kind of autumn John missed in Florida. John told his dad how sorry he was that he had been a disappointment to them, that he had not gone into the ministry or completed college. But he assured his dad that in every church he had been in, he had always mowed the lawn for the pastor just as he had mowed their lawn as a boy. He had been the maintenance man in every church as well as a bulwark of support for the pastor. He had always made sure the pastor never went without.

Floyd looked at his son and John could tell he was not disappointed a bit. Floyd said, "I know that, son, and I am as proud of you as I am of anything in this world. Remember this, I just wanted you to be your best self and to give it all you've got and you have done that!" John shared this story at Grandpa's funeral and then sang the old Irish song *Heaven will be Heaven because I will see my dad!*

This is all that I can tell about their heart wounds, because in Grandma's words I was a pastor first. I can say that as far as they were concerned, they felt all their boys loved them, and forgave them for their every failing.

One Sunday night when I preached in my dad's church, my grandpa came to hear me. Before I was done he stood up and announced that he wanted to add something. He said God was very good to him throughout his life, even though he had made his share of mistakes. The very best blessing of many blessings was a lovely wife who always loved him and six tiny boys that made him feel like he could change the world all by himself. Three of their boys are clergymen, one is a retired steel construction superintendent who now works at a Christian retreat center, one is a government welfare department employee, and another is a physicist. Floyd and Ione were extremely proud of each of them as well as each and every grandchild and great-grandchild.

One day after a work session on this book, Grandpa and I took a walk. He said he wanted me to know that he never would have done or been anything if it hadn't been for some very Godly lay-people in the church who had stood by him every time there was a challenge. After saying this, he cried like a little boy, saying that God always sent him the right friend at the right time and he would like me to thank each and every one of them for him. They are all in heaven now, so I guess he is thanking them himself right now.

What do you say about the heart wounds acquired over the years by human beings? One story that may say it best was when Floyd was communicating for someone else.

There was a feeling of awe in the country church as their admired former pastor, Floyd White, walked up to the casket with the old, old woman in it. He touched her hand — how he loved his people. He turned and read the obituary with a touch of disgust, because it was so short and glib. The pastor spoke with emotion in his voice. This was an issue that he had chosen. He had a point to make. "I know most people think that this old woman's life never amounted to much. She had her imperfections. She didn't have a family, never had any money, in fact most of you probably don't even remember a day when she didn't live in the old folks home. Those of you who do remember her know that a lot of people made fun of how old and cranky she was; she was old even when I was young. People would make fun of how the widow was behind the times — and they were right! There was nothing flashy about her, and a lot of the younger generation just could not understand her 'uniqueness', that would be a nice way to put it. You probably think that her life never mattered. Let me tell you, it mattered — it mattered!

"I knew the widow and she was a fine Christian in every way. When there was a family having to do without she would bring me food from her garden to give to them as long as I kept her name anonymous. Some of your grandparents got by that way. At Christmas it was the same story. How many of you received an anonymous Christmas present or food at hard times? I'm here to tell you it was the widow who sent me to give them to you.

"And she was always there at every church meeting. She never missed, and that was an encouragement to me. She taught the preschool Sunday school class for generations. No one else wanted it. She taught the little ones about God's love and how to pray. How many of you here today were in her Sunday school class? Stand up!" The crowd looked around nervously as first a ranch hand, then a dignified storeowner, and then a housewife stood up, all with tears running down their cheeks. Before it was over three-fourths of the congregation was standing.

Floyd went on, "When we didn't have a church bell, the widow said, 'A church just has to have a bell.' And she raised the money. It took her a few years, but she did it with the help of the Sunday school kids. Her life is like that old bell."

The old pastor walked to the back of the church, grabbed the rope, and pulled with all his might. For a few minutes he stood there ringing the bell. As he let go of the rope and the bell's sound quieted, he raised his hand for a blessing as he had done for so many years and he prayed with his old voice over the sound of the bell.

> *May the bell keep on ringing.*
> *May the lives keep on singing.*
> *This was a great old lady*
> *for the Almighty truly worked in her life!!!*
> *Amen and Amen*

A prayer by Rev. Floyd E. White:

Dear Father God, when the shadows fall and the darkness, may our hope in Christ remain steadfast and sure. Give us tender concern and respect for all people everywhere. May we become aware of their beauty and see through their roughness to see the diamond lying there waiting. In the name of the One who is, as St. John has written, "the Light of the World."

Amen and Amen.

CHAPTER TEN

Lessons
From Grandpa

6.2 billion in 2000

December 21, 1986

According to statistics just released by the Census Bureau, the world population is reproducing itself more slowly now than it was in the early 1960s. But not slowly enough. By the year 2000, about 170 cities in the world will have over two million residents. Three-fourths of the population will live in developing countries, and many of those people will be elderly. The number of people in the world age 64 and over will increase 46 percent. And the total global population will likely increase 27 percent in the next 14 years to reach 6.2 billion. The problem is with all of us.

Chronicle of the 20th Century, Chronicle Publications,
Mount Kisco, New York, 1987, page 1291

We now have only 3 percent of the information that will be available to us by the year 2010.

George Barna, The Frog in the Kettle, Regal Books,
Ventura, California, 1990, page 49

The gradual changes of the 90s — the result of three decades of ferment — will hit with full force by 2000.

George Barna, page 30

Today's values — affluence, self, short-term commitments and quality; tomorrow's skepticism about other people and institutions, suspicious of traditions.

George Barna, page 30

By 2000, Americans will generally believe that a life spent with the same partner is both unusual and unnecessary.

George Barna, page 71

"The traditional family is dead!" "We have become a nation of friendless adults." "Marriage is an outdated institution." Read any magazine or newspaper article about the days ahead, and you are likely to encounter such dramatic statments. While some journalists have exaggerated the state of affairs regarding the family and friendships in America, they have captured the spirit of the changes likely in the next decade.

George Barna, page 66

The real issue behind quotas will be the future of affirmative action. As the 1990s move forward, minorities striving to rise and whites struggling not to sink are going to be asking the same questions: who helps you when you don't get your fair share, and just who is the little guy now?

Tom Matthews, Newsweek,
December 31, 1990, page 29

Reform scenarios are a dime a dozen, and some skeptics think U.S. education is in danger of suffocating under the avalanche of earnest white papers that have promulgated over the past decade. There is much talk, for example, of the need for restructuring the public school system.

Tom Morganthau, Newsweek,
December 31, 1990, page 35

Germany and Japan will have nuclear weapons by the year 2000. Unless the U.S. agrees to defend them, Arab nations will also buy nukes.

Evan Thomas, Newsweek,
December 31, 1990, page 18

Lessons From Grandpa

*"Help me, friend Sancho, to get up
into the enchanted chariot again;"*

CERVANTES, *The Ingenious Gentleman
Don Quixote De La Mancha*

What about our generation? At the end of Grandpa's life there were no brave last words for the coming generation. There was not a financial inheritance, only a shoebox full of sermons from 1933, 1944, 1953, and 1968. In fact, he left only the unspoken question, "Did we get the point?"

I spoke at his funeral with six other ministers, and afterwards I walked to Grandpa and Grandma's simple gravestone with their life verse on it.

I will lift my eyes to the hills from whence cometh my strength, my strength cometh from the Lord the maker of heaven and earth.

At that moment my mind raced with thoughts of how very different the twenty-first century would be from Grandpa's century.

Today there is inflation instead of depression. Fundamentalist and Liberal now have different meanings. Republican and Democrat, Communist, and free enterprise, all mean something very different. Traffic jams, computer viruses, and junk bonds meant nothing in Grandpa's century. We're beyond negative doomsayers, such as George Orwell's *1984*, the classic novel which presented a dark view of the future when it was written in 1949.

I am a pastor in a city with yuppies and street gangs, car telephones and smog. What wars will the little boys in my church have to grow up to fight? What financial storms will the couples have to brave after I perform their weddings? The world of the twenty-first century is very different from the 1890s of Grandpa's childhood.

Somehow in this stark contrast between the centuries, the lessons from our grandparents ring out more clearly. Obviously they did not have all the answers. Some of the answers we will have to find for ourselves, but the few foundational lessons they have taught are a good place for us to start. Their simple ways give us a melody that will take away the fear of the shadows seemingly cast upon the days to come. Homespun principles bring a rhythm to life and a smile to the face! I think you will discover these precepts are a place to stand, a chart to follow, and a sense of home where you may find rest. We now live in a century that most certainly needs a sense of home.

Everyone needs a grandpa and a grandma, and this book represents some of the lessons I learned from mine. I hope that you can share in them, and more importantly, come to understand that someday your grandchild may be writing a book like this about your life.

When I was attending theological seminary, my dad, my grandpa, and I stood in the backyard watering flowers. Dad commented to Grandpa, "Did you know Tim received straight A's in seminary?"

"Well, that's wonderful," Grandpa replied. "I wonder where he got it." He paused and asked, "How did you do in school, Dale?"

Dad answered tearfully, as both of them realized that Grandpa had been too busy to know how his fourth son had done in school.

"Pretty good," my dad said. "I got straight A's in the 5th grade at Greenwood Elementary School."

Then Grandpa began to be covered with a wave of deep remorse for everything he had missed with his boys. "I guess I never noticed," he said as he cried.

Then, because my dad knew Jesus, he responded and forgave his dad and put his arm around him. "That's all right; you noticed now, didn't you?"

Grandpa smiled as he hugged Dad, "Good job in the 5th grade at Greenwood Elementary School!" For a moment, before my very eyes, my dad was a little boy and my grandpa was a young man. All of this came through the power of the wonderful God that Grandpa had served throughout his life.

Later that evening, Grandpa and I returned again to the deck in the backyard. The sunset illuminated the land with radiant beauty and effulgent lights. Everything glowed bright orange, reflecting the sunset. Grandpa took a deep breath of the fresh country air with the scent of pine and flowers intermingled. He closed his eyes and spoke slowly, with almost a century of emotion behind each word. "God is so good. Life is so short. It's such a precious gift."

Then he turned to me and said, "What do you hear, Tim?"

I listened. "Nothing, Grandpa."

He repeated softly and almost sounded like Dr. Collister. "Listen!"

"I heard it that time, Grandpa. It's a bird singing."

He asked, and I knew he was trying to teach me something. "Why is it singing?"

I thought. I don't know why birds sing, so I guessed. "Because he is hungry?"

He looked at me as if he was wondering if I would ever learn. Then he spoke to me with all the gusto he could muster. "Because he's alive and there is a lot to sing about!"

That was the way it was around Grandpa all the time in the later years of his life. But I was not always aware of the greatness in this common man. We are all surrounded by great people if we will just learn to look and listen!

I have wondered when it was that I began to discover the grandeur in Grandpa's life. Maybe it was when the celebrated author Alex Haley delivered my college graduation address. He told us, "There are great stories in the common ordinary people of life. They may not see it themselves; nevertheless, it is there underneath the surface. To discover it we must search with an eye of faith." Alex Haley was inspirational and insightful. His address was timely, but that was not the beginning of my appreciation for my grandfather.

When I was a boy, my family was traveling across northern Oregon heading to the Rose Festival in Portland, Oregon. At a truck stop in Umatilla, Oregon, an old rancher stopped my dad after reading the name imprinted on his check, which said "Reverend White."

He asked, "Are you related to Reverend Floyd White?"

Dad said, "Yes, I am one of his boys."

The rancher acted like we were all royalty as he exclaimed, "Reverend Floyd White is the greatest person I have ever had the privilege to meet in my life! You can take General Eisenhower or that Mahatma Gandhi, but in our territory, it is Reverend White!" My dad laughed at the overstatement, knowing that was the way people talked in that part of the country.

The man saw the smile on Dad's face and said, "Now listen here, sonny, I mean it! Years ago I was not only bound for hell, but I brought hell with me everywhere I went! I hated Christians and especially preachers. My wife and children up and started attending the Methodist Church when Floyd White moved to town. That really made me mad! Preachers were the bur under my saddle with their condemnation and useless heavenly minded thinking."

As the rancher told the story, we could all picture him being a rough person. He smiled like a cowboy as he said, "One day after a storm, a tree fell across the road outside our farm house. It upset me that there was no one who felt responsible to help me clear that tree. I was out there cussing, trying to work a two-man saw on that tree. Anyone who has ever worked a two-man saw knows it can be pretty frustrating when you are working by yourself."

He spoke now with frustration. "As I was just about as dad-blamed frustrated as I could get, I saw Pastor White walking down the road. In those days, preachers all had to wear the same black suits. I guess that was so the townspeople could see them coming and quit telling any off-color jokes, or having any of the wrong kind of fun before the preacher arrived. It was kind of a built-in alarm system."

The rancher told us that the closer Pastor White walked, the angrier he became. Finally, he decided to himself that if the preacher said one word, he would just deck him.

He started to get tears in his eyes as he told us, "As Reverend White arrived he just looked me in the eye, like he was unafraid but genuinely cared. He just took off his coat and started working the other side of the saw without saying a word until the job was done." Then the rancher invited him in for a cup of coffee. When he finally visited church, he realized that everything about that country preacher, from his practical messages to his calls when people went through hardship, was just working the other side of a two-sided saw for people.

The rancher with leathery skin told us, "That may not sound like much to most folks, but I'm a Christian today because I met a real Christian named Reverend White."

After Grandpa died, I couldn't help but rewrite an old poem by Chaucer entitled *The Good Parson*. Except for a few phrases, my rewrite looks very little like the original. I entitled it *The Country Pastor*.

The pastor of a country valley was he,
    who knew something of humble poverty.
But he was rich in lofty thought,
    caring gently as he taught.
He worked for Jesus diligent,
    and in tough times still content.
The good news of Christ most powerfully did he preach,
    and Godly values did he devoutly teach.

To all his flock he was a friend,
   no way — would he put down or contend.
Of his own would he always give,
   Content on little for himself to live.
Sorrow and sickness won his kindly care;
   with Bible in hand he traveled everywhere.
This good example to his flock he brought,
   that first he worked and then he taught.
The shepherd's example was clear to give,
   by his encouragement others would live.
He did not put his ideals to hire,
   and leave his sheep trapped in the mire.
He would spend his life watching his flock to keep,
   from prowling wolves he would protect his sheep.
Not sparing of his speech in vain conceit,
   but in his teaching being kind and discreet.
He drew his flock to heaven with noble art,
   by encouragement and love straight from his heart.
Always when it looked like he was down,
   he would look up and reach for a crown.
His eyes were so tender, his touch was mild,
   his priority was always one child.
Love, an encouraging word, was all that was sown;
   but it was obvious they weren't his own.
Sometimes his dreams would fail and we would see his shame,
   but then we would hear his heart and remember that
   Pastor was his name.
The moments would pass quickly
   through the struggle of years.
Many of our precious victories
   were seen through our tears.
Farewell then, all the world, Adieu,
   The country pastor has been there for you.

Grandpa was always there, but the moment I discovered him was on a day when I was not looking. It was 1972, when I was a senior in high school. My mom asked me to pick up Grandpa and drive him to Basin Surplus to get some new shoes. I felt put out. He was so eccentric, and I was a big-time football player. I felt embarrassed to walk next to my old grandpa while I was wearing my impressive letterman's jacket.

When we walked into the store, immediately I knew we were in trouble. There, standing in the middle of the store, was a mountain of a man. He was at least six foot six inches tall. He was a biker and he looked like he would kill you if you looked at him. He had a Fu Manchu mustache and was smoking a big green cigar. I remember his huge, rippling bicep had some ugly tattoo on it.

As we stepped in the store, we heard this loud slap as we saw him strike his little boy hard enough to knock him silly. He turned as if he were going to hit his sleazy-looking wife, and profanities erupted from him. More evil radiated from that "Hell's Angel" than I had ever seen in my life.

Everyone in the store was hiding. This guy was so rough I think even Clint Eastwood would have looked the other way. I was thinking about the same thing when I saw my grandpa raise his head and square his jaw. I grabbed his shoulder holding him back and said, "Grandpa, nobody expects it!"

He turned to me, looking like a cowboy who could see in the little boy with a handprint on his face another little Ephraim. "I expect it," he said.

Being a tough football player, I hid behind a clothes rack. Grandpa walked across the store looking like a sheriff going to a showdown against a deadly gunfighter, as if he were making a stand and saying, "Not in my town."

I didn't know it then, but as I think back about it now, Grandpa demonstrated such courage in that moment that his mind must have been flashing back, remembering what it felt like to be a little boy, alone at the age of 10. Remembering Dr. Collister and the talk after the hanging, remembering how God worked through Old Cap to bring him to the Methodist Church in Sweet, Idaho, remembering Ione's speech to him when they left for New Meadows or the time that he had wanted to quit, remembering the brave lay people who had stood by his side as they dreamed together.

"Wohhhhh, what is going on over here?" He stepped up and began to squeeze the elbow of the biker. Grandpa was grinning as he told one of the silly jokes he was always telling. Then he told the biker about the football game at New Meadows and what a fix he had been in, and how the Lord had helped him. The biker began to smile behind his big green cigar at the humor, sincerity, and courage of this country pastor.

Grandpa complimented him on his biceps, his wife's beauty, and how this boy would probably grow up and do something really great. Everyone in the store was listening to the conversation and chuckling at my grandpa's ridiculous but sincere idealism. Then he raised his hand to give them a benediction. The surgery was about to begin and he would say things in prayer that no one else could get away with saying. There was such honesty, humility, and love when he prayed that it was just a sight to see!

He prayed out loud in that Charlton Heston voice. "And now, Jesus, touch these good people with your mighty love. Only you know the deep hurts in all of our lives and I pray that you will give them a new start through your amazing forgiveness displayed on the cross — put back fear and anger and give them gentleness at this moment so that they will know it is coming from you, the author of love and life."

A power capsule
inspired by Romans 4:17-21

As it is written: "I have made you a father of many nations."
He is our father in the sight of God, in whom he believed —
the God who gives life to the dead and calls things that are not
as though they were. Against all hope, Abraham in hope
believed and so became the father of many nations, just as it
had been said to him, 'So shall your offspring be.' Without
weakening in his faith, he faced the fact that his body was as
good as dead —since he was about a hundred years old —
and that Sarah's womb was also dead. Yet he did not
waver through unbelief regarding the promise of God, but was
strengthened in his faith and gave glory to God, being fully
persuaded that God had power to do what he promised.

When you pray, claim what isn't as if it were, 'til it becomes!

(Become fully persuaded that God has
power to do what he has promised.)

Grandpa continued to pray, but his eyes were the only ones that were closed. Everyone in the store was staring, wondering what had just happened. I know I was wondering. It was a phenomenon to behold. Something had transformed that situation. People were staring as if they had just watched a miracle. The sight was incredible. The biker was smiling peacefully as Grandpa prayed for him.

It was as if the evil in this man had been bound, and a new man had been set free. The child with the red mark on his face had his mouth wide open, staring at Grandpa. His mother had tears streaking down her face as she also was wondering about the identity of this old man. They must have suspected that God himself was shining through this "diamond in the rough." If you were there, you would have seen that there was love flowing from a well-worn channel that had been blasted clear by deep hurts in the past. Grandpa had somehow found healing through God's grace, and he had experienced it continually over the years. Where once a cold river of loneliness flowed, a warm river called grace now blessed everyone he met.

So many people who met my grandpa have commented to me that he was an uncommon man. I usually tell them, "Thank you, but not really. He was just a common uncommon Christian!" There are millions of quiet heroes like him all over the world. If we learn to watch them carefully and listen attentively, we can begin to follow the One they are following! Then we will discover the humble grandeur our Creator has placed in every life!

Here's to the country doctor and the simple pastor that he trained!

Here's to the man who spends his life working with winos at the Union Gospel Mission and nobody notices!

Here's to the hard laborers who raise their families by the sweat of their brow!

Here's to the schoolteachers who spend their lives working with kids, helping them to be the best that they can be, with very few returns to say "thank you!"

Here's to the single mom who gets up with her baby in the middle of the night. That baby will never remember!

Here's to the soldiers who died in battle protecting our freedom, and many drive by the graveyard and never notice!

Here's to the immigrant farm workers who laid the foundation for the next generation!

Here's to the parents who work so their children can go through college and have a better life!

Here's to the cop working a lonely beat!

Here's to the single dad who makes time for his kids in spite of the personal pain he feels every time he has to tell them good-bye!

Here's to all the grandpas and grandmas who make the special effort to discover the glory, grandeur and adventure of loving greatly, being genuine, and believing superbly in all those who have had the courage to observe their lives!

And here's to every person who is doing great things, not because they will be noticed, but because it is the right thing to do!

Here's to all the Dreamers Long Forgotten, and all those who don't need this book to follow their path!

> *…which leads us to hope that we may be given an account of Don Quixote's third sally.*
>
> CERVANTES, *The Ingenious Gentleman Don Quixote De La Mancha*